VISITS
TO THE
BLESSED
SACRAMENT
AND OUR LADY

Blessed be Jesus in the Most Holy
Sacrament of the Altar.

VISITS
TO THE
BLESSED
SACRAMENT
AND OUR LADY

By

St. Alphonsus Liguori

*Re-edited from the critical Italian edition
and newly written into English (c. 1952) by
The Redemptorist Fathers*

TAN BOOKS AND PUBLISHERS, INC.
Rockford, Illinois 61105

Imprimi Potest: Michael Curran, C.SS.R.
Provincial Superior
Limerick
October 23, 1952

Imprimi Potest: ✠ Patrick
Bishop of Limerick
Limerick
November 1, 1952

Published in Ireland around 1952. Retypeset and republished in 2000 by TAN Books and Publishers, Inc., with permission of the Redemptorist Provincial, Dublin.

Fontispiece courtesy of Discalced Carmelite Nuns, Danvers, Massachusetts.

Library of Congress Control No.: 00-131561

ISBN 0-89555-667-7

Printed and bound in the United States of America.

TAN BOOKS AND PUBLISHERS, INC.
P.O. Box 424
Rockford, Illinois 61105

2000

Dedication To Our Lady

By The Author

MY most holy Queen, on the point of publishing the present little work, which treats of the love of your Son, I know not to whom I can better dedicate it than to you, my most beloved Mother, who, among all creatures, are His greatest lover. I believe that in making to you this little offering of a work composed for the sole purpose of inflaming souls more and more with the love of Jesus Christ I shall greatly please you, who desire to see Him loved by everyone as He deserves. To you, then, I consecrate it, such as it is; do you graciously accept and watch over it, not indeed that I may receive the praises of men, but that all who read it may, for the future, correspond by their greater devotion and affection to the tender, the excessive love which our most sweet Saviour has been pleased to show us in His Passion and in the institution of the Most Holy Sacrament. As such, I place it at your feet and beseech you to accept, as entirely yours, both the gift and the giver, who has long since placed all his hope in you and wishes and hopes ever to call himself, and to rejoice in being,

Most gracious Lady,

Your most loving, though most unworthy servant,

ALPHONSUS DE LIGUORI.

CONTENTS

Instructions On The Visits

These Instructions are from the edition of the Visits *published sometime between 1907-1944 by Mission Church Press, Boston, with the Imprimatur of William [O'Connell], Archbishop of Boston. The above heading and the Instruction subheadings were added by the present publisher, 2000.*

The Visit To The
Most Blessed Sacrament

OUR holy Faith teaches us, and we are bound to believe, that in the consecrated Host Jesus Christ is really present under the species of bread. But we must also understand that He is thus present on our altars as on a throne of love and mercy, to dispense graces and there to show us the love which He bears us by being pleased to dwell night and day hidden in the midst of us.

It is well known that the Holy Church instituted the festival of Corpus Christi with a solemn octave, and that she celebrates it with the many usual processions and such frequent expositions of this Most Holy Sacrament, that men may thereby be moved gratefully to acknowledge and honor this loving presence and dwelling of Jesus Christ in the

Sacrament of the Altar by their devotions, thanksgivings and the tender affections of their souls. O God, how many insults and outrages has not this amiable Redeemer had, and does He not have daily, to endure in this Sacrament on the part of those very men for whose love He remains upon their altars on earth! Of this He indeed complained to His dear servant Sister Margaret Alacoque [St. Margaret Mary], as the author of the *Book of Devotion to the Heart of Jesus* relates:

The Heart of Jesus

One day, as she was in prayer before the Most Holy Sacrament, Jesus showed her His Heart on a throne of flames, crowned with thorns and surmounted by a cross, and thus He addressed her: "Behold that Heart which has loved men so much, and which has spared itself nothing, and has even gone so far as to consume itself, thereby to show them its love; but in return the greater part of men show Me only ingratitude, and this by irreverence, tepidity, sacrileges and contempt which they offer Me in this Sacrament of love; and that which I feel the most acutely is that they are hearts consecrated to Me." Jesus then expressed His wish that the first Friday after the octave of Corpus Christi should be dedicated as a particular festival in honor of His adorable Heart, and that on that day all souls who loved Him should endeavor, by their homage and by the affections of their souls, to make amends for the insults which men have offered Him in this Sacrament of the Altar; and at the same time He promised abundant graces to all who should thus honor Him.

We can thus understand what Our Lord said of old by His prophet: that His delight is to be with the children of men (*Prov.* 8:31), since He is unable to tear Himself from them even when they abandon and despise Him. This also shows us how agreeable to the Heart of Jesus are all those souls who frequently visit Him and remain in His company in the churches in which He is under the sacramental species. He desired St. Mary Magdalene of Pazzi to visit Him in the Most Blessed Sacrament 33 times a day; this beloved spouse of His faithfully obeyed Him and, in all her visits to the altar, approached it as near as she possibly could, as we read in her Life.

Saints and the Blessed Sacrament

But let all those devout souls who often go to spend their time with the Most Blessed Sacrament speak: let them tell us the gifts, the inspirations which they have received, the flames of love which are there enkindled in their souls, the paradise which they enjoy in the presence of this hidden God.

The servant of God and great Sicilian missionary, Father Louis La Nusa, was, even in his youth and as a layman, so enamored of Jesus Christ that he seemed unable to tear himself from the presence of his beloved Lord. Such were the joys which he there experienced that his director commanded him, in virtue of obedience, not to remain there for more than an hour. The time having elapsed, he showed in obeying (says the author of his Life) that in tearing himself from the bosom of Jesus Christ he had to do himself just such violence as a child that has to detach itself from its mother's breast in the very moment in which it is satiating itself with the utmost avidity; and when he had to do this, we are told that he remained standing with his eyes fixed on the altar, making repeated inclinations, as if he knew not how to leave his Lord, whose presence was so sweet and gracious to him.

"Depart from me, O Lord!"

To St. Aloysius it was also forbidden to remain in the presence of the Most Blessed Sacrament; and as he used to pass before it, finding himself drawn, so to speak, by the sweet attractions of his Lord and almost forced to remain there, he would tear himself away with the greatest effort, saying with an excess of tender love: "Depart from me, O Lord, depart!" There it was also that St. Francis Xavier found refreshment in the midst of his many labors in India, for he employed his days toiling for souls and his nights in the presence of the Most Blessed Sacrament. St. John Francis Regis did the same thing: and sometimes finding the church closed, he endeavored to satisfy his longings by remaining on his knees outside the door, exposed to the rain or cold, that at least at a distance he might attend upon his Comforter concealed under the sacramental species.

Good King Wenceslaus

St. Francis of Assisi used to go to communicate all his labors and undertakings to Jesus in the Most Holy Sacrament. But tender indeed was the devotion to the Most Blessed Sacrament of St. Wenceslaus, Duke of Bohemia. This holy king was so enamored of Jesus there present that he not only gathered wheat and grapes and made the hosts and wine with his own hands and then gave them to be used in the Holy Sacrifice, but even during the winter he used to go at night to visit the church in which the Blessed Sacrament was kept. These visits enkindled in his beautiful soul such flames of divine love that their ardor imparted itself even to his body and took from the snow on which he walked its wonted cold; for it is related that the servant who accompanied him in these nightly excursions, having to walk through the snow, suffered much from the cold. The holy King, on perceiving this, was moved to compassion and commanded him to follow him and only to step in his footmarks; he did so, and never afterwards felt the cold.

Your Most Profitable Time Spent

In the Visits you will read other examples of the tender affection with which souls inflamed with the love of God loved to dwell in the presence of the Most Holy Sacrament. But you will find that all the Saints were enamored of this most sweet devotion since, indeed, it is impossible to find on earth a more precious gem or a treasure more worthy of all our love than Jesus in the Most Holy Sacrament.

Certainly, among all devotions after that of receiving the Sacraments, that of adoring Jesus in the Blessed Sacrament holds first place, is the most pleasing to God and the most useful to ourselves. Do not then, O devout soul, refuse to begin this devotion; and forsaking the conversation of men, dwell each day, from this time forward, for at least a half or quarter of an hour in some church in the presence of Jesus Christ under the sacramental species. *O taste, and see that the Lord is sweet. (Ps.* 33:9). Only try this devotion, and by experience you will see the great benefit that you will derive from it. Be assured that the time you will thus spend with devotion before this most divine Sacrament will be the most profitable to you in life and the source of your greatest consolation in death and in eternity.

You must also be aware that in a quarter of an hour's prayer spent in the presence of the Blessed Sacrament, you will perhaps gain more than in all the other spiritual exercises of the day. It is true that in every place God graciously hears the petitions of those who pray to Him, having promised to do so: *Ask, and you shall receive (John* 16:24); yet the disciple tells us that Jesus dispenses His graces in greater abundance to those who visit Him in the Most Holy Sacrament.

St. Alphonsus' Own Testimony

Blessed Henry of Suso also used to say that Jesus Christ hears the prayers of the faithful more graciously in the Sacrament of the

Altar than elsewhere. And where, indeed, did holy souls make their most beautiful resolutions but prostrate before the Most Holy Sacrament? Who knows but that you also may one day, in the presence of the Tabernacle, make the resolution to give yourself entirely to God? In this little book I feel bound, at least out of gratitude to my Jesus in the Holy Sacrament, to declare that through the means of this devotion of visiting the Most Blessed Sacrament, which I practiced, though with so much tepidity and in so imperfect a manner, I abandoned the world, in which, unfortunately, I lived until I was six-and-twenty years of age. Fortunate indeed will you be if you can detach yourself from it at an earlier period and give yourself without reserve to that Lord who has given Himself without reserve to you.

"Taste and See"

I repeat that indeed you will be blessed, not only in eternity, but even in this life. Believe me, all is folly: feasts, theaters, parties of pleasure, amusements—these are the goods of this world, but goods which are filled with the bitterness of gall and with sharp thorns. Believe me, who have experienced this and now weep over it. Be also assured that Jesus Christ finds means to console a soul that remains with a recollected spirit before the Most Blessed Sacrament, far beyond what the world can do with all its feasts and pastimes.

Oh, how sweet a joy it is to remain with faith and tender devotion before an altar and converse familiarly with Jesus Christ, who is there for the express purpose of listening to and graciously hearing those who pray to Him; to ask His pardon for the displeasure which we have caused Him; to represent our wants to Him, as a friend does to a friend in whom he places all his confidence; to ask Him for His graces, for His love and for His kingdom; but above all—oh, what a heaven it is to remain there making acts of love toward that Lord who is on the very altar praying to the Eternal Father for us and is there burning with love for us! Indeed, that love it is which detains Him there, thus hidden and unknown, and when He is even despised by ungrateful souls! But why should we say more? "Taste and see."

On Spiritual Communion

AS in all the following Visits to the Most Blessed Sacrament a Spiritual Communion is recommended, it will be well to explain what it is and the great advantages which result from its practice. A Spiritual Communion, according to St. Thomas, consists in an ardent desire to receive Jesus in the Most Holy Sacrament and in lovingly embracing Him as if we had actually received Him. How pleasing these Spiritual Communions are to God and the many graces which He bestows through their means was manifested by Our Lord Himself to Sister Paula Maresca, the foundress of the convent of St. Catherine of Siena in Naples, when (as it is related in her Life) He showed her two precious vessels, the one of gold, the other of silver; He then told her that in the gold vessel He preserved her sacramental Communions, and in the silver one her Spiritual Communions. He also told Blessed Jane of the Cross that each time she communicated spiritually she received a grace of the same kind as the one that she received when she really communicated. Above all, it will suffice for us to know that the holy Council of Trent greatly praises Spiritual Communions and encourages the faithful to practice them. (Sess. 13, c. 8).

Hence all devout souls are accustomed often to practice this holy exercise of Spiritual Communion. Blessed Agatha of the Cross did so 200 times a day. And Father Peter Faber, the first companion of St. Ignatius, used to say that it was of the highest use-fulness to make Spiritual Communions in order to receive sacramental Communion well.

All those who desire to advance in the love of Jesus Christ are exhorted to make a Spiritual Communion at least once in every visit that they pay to the Most Blessed Sacrament, and at every Mass that they hear; and it would even be better on these occasions to repeat the Communions three times, that is to say, at the beginning, in the middle and at the end. This devotion is far more profitable than some suppose, and at the same time nothing can be easier in practice. The above-named Blessed Jane of the Cross used to say that a Spiritual Communion can be made without anyone noticing it, without being fasting, without the permission of our director, and that we can make it at any time we please: an act of love does all.

An Act Of Spiritual Communion

My Jesus, I believe that Thou art present in the Most Blessed Sacrament. I love Thee above all things, and I desire to receive Thee into my soul. Since I cannot now receive Thee sacramentally, come at least spiritually into my heart. I embrace Thee as if Thou wert

already come, and unite myself wholly to
Thee. Never permit me to be separated from
Thee. Amen.

A Shorter Act

O Jesus, I believe that Thou art in the Most
Blessed Sacrament! Come into my heart. I
embrace Thee; oh, never leave me!

"May the burning and most sweet power of
Thy love, O Lord Jesus Christ, I beseech
Thee, absorb my mind, that I may die through
love of Thy love, Who was graciously pleased
to die through love of my love."—*St. Francis
of Assisi*

"O love not loved! O love not known!"—*St.
Mary Magdalene of Pazzi*

"O my Spouse, when wilt Thou take me to
Thyself?"—*St. Peter of Alcantara*

Jesus, my Good, my sweetest Love,
Strike and inflame this heart of mine,
Make it all fire for love of Thee!

Hail to the love of Jesus, our life and our
all! Hail to Mary, our hope! Amen.

After the Spiritual Communion, you will then make a visit to some image of the Blessed Virgin Mary.

The Visit To The Blessed Virgin

AND now as to the visits to the Most Blessed Virgin, the opinion of St. Bernard is well known and generally believed: it is that God dispenses no graces otherwise than through the hands of Mary: "God wills that we should receive nothing that does not pass through Mary's hands." (*In Vig. Nat. Dom.*, s. 3). Hence Father Suarez declares that it is now the sentiment of the universal Church that "the intercession of Mary is not only useful, but even necessary to obtain graces." (*De Inc.*, p. 2, p. 37, a. 4, d. 23). And we may remark that the Church gives us strong grounds for this belief by applying the words of the Sacred Scripture to Mary and making her say: *In me is all hope of life and of virtue. Come over to me, all ye that desire me . . .* (*Ecclus.* 24:25). Let all come to me; for I am the hope of all that you can desire. Hence she then adds: *Blessed is the man that heareth me, and that watcheth daily at my gates, and waiteth at the posts of my doors.* (*Prov.* 8:34). Blessed is he who is diligent in coming every day to the door of my powerful intercession; for by finding me he will find life and eternal salvation: *He that shall find me, shall find life, and shall have salvation from the Lord.* (*Prov.* 8:35). Hence it is not without reason that the Holy Church wills that we should call her our common hope by saluting her, saying, "Hail, our hope!"

"Let us then," says St. Bernard (who went so far as to call Mary "the whole ground of his hope"), "seek for graces, and seek them through Mary." (*De Aquaed.*). Otherwise, says St. Antonius, if we ask for graces without her intercession, we shall be making an effort to fly without wings, and we shall obtain nothing. "He who asks without her as his guide attempts to fly without wings." (P. 4, tit. 15, c. 22).

Graces Obtained through Visits to The Blessed Virgin Mary

In Father Auriemma's little book, *Affetti Scambievoli* (p. 2, c. 3), we read of innumerable favors granted by the Mother of God to those who practiced this most profitable devotion of often visiting her in her churches or before some image. We read of the graces which she granted in these visits to Blessed Albert the Great, to the Abbot Rupert, to Father Suarez—especially when she obtained for them the gift of understanding, by which they afterward became so renowned throughout the Church for their great learning. We read of the graces which she granted to the Venerable [now St.] John Berchmans of the Society of Jesus, who was in the daily habit of visiting Mary in a chapel of the Roman College; he declared that he renounced all earthly love, to love no other after God than the Most Blessed Virgin, and he had written at the foot of an image of his beloved Lady: "I will never rest until I shall have obtained a tender love for my Mother." We read also of the graces which she granted to St. Bernardine of Siena, who in his youth also went every day to visit her in a chapel near the city gate and declared that that Lady had ravished his heart. Hence he called her his beloved and said that he could not do less than visit her often; and by her means he afterward obtained the grace to renounce the world and to become what he afterward was, a great Saint and the apostle of Italy.

Do you, then, be also careful always to join to your daily visit to the Most Blessed Sacrament a visit to the most holy Virgin Mary in some church, or at least before a devout image of her in your own house. If you do this with tender affection and confidence, you may hope to receive great things from this most

gracious Lady, who, as St. Andrew of Crete
says, always bestows great gifts on those who
offer her even the least act of homage. (*In
Dorm. B. V.*, s. 3).

Mary, Queen of sweetest hope,
Who can e'er forget thee?
By thy mercy, by thy love,
Have pity, Queen, on me!

VISITS
TO THE
BLESSED
SACRAMENT
AND OUR LADY

How To Make A Visit

1. Introductory Prayer: "My Lord Jesus Christ . . ." (Page 1).

2. Visit to the Blessed Sacrament, corresponding to day of the month.

3. Spiritual Communion. (Page 2).

4. Visit to Our Lady, corresponding to day of the month.

5. Prayer to Our Lady: "Most holy Virgin Immaculate . . ." (Page 3).

Prayer Before Each Visit

MY LORD Jesus Christ, Who because of Your love for men remain night and day in the Blessed Sacrament, full of pity and of love, awaiting, calling and welcoming all who come to visit You, I believe that You are present here on the altar. I adore You, and I thank You for all the graces You have bestowed on me, especially for having given me Yourself in this Sacrament, for having given me Your most holy Mother Mary to plead for me, and for having called me to visit You in this church. I now salute Your most loving Heart, and that for three ends: 1) in thanksgiving for this great gift; 2) to make amends to You for all the outrages committed against You in this Sacrament by Your enemies; 3) I intend by this visit to adore You in all the places on earth in which You are present in the Blessed Sacrament and in which You are least honored and most abandoned.

My Jesus, I love You with my whole heart. I am very sorry for having so many times offended Your infinite goodness. With the help of Your grace, I purpose never to offend You again. And now, unworthy though I am, I consecrate myself to You without reserve. I renounce and give entirely to You my will, my affection, my desires and all that I possess. For the future, dispose of me and all I have as You please. All I ask of You is Your holy love, final perseverance and that I may carry out Your will perfectly. I recommend to You the souls in Purgatory, especially those who had the greatest devotion to the Blessed Sacrament and to the Blessed Virgin Mary. I also recommend to You all poor sinners. Finally, my dear Saviour, I unite all my desires with the desires of Your most loving Heart; and I offer them, thus united, to the Eternal Father, and beseech Him, in Your name and for love of You, to accept and grant them.

Spiritual Communion

My Jesus, I believe that You are present in the Most Blessed Sacrament. I love You above all things, and I desire to receive You into my soul. Since I cannot now receive You sacramentally, come at least spiritually into my heart. I embrace You as if You were already come, and I unite myself wholly to You. Never permit me to be separated from You.

Prayer To Our Lady
After Each Visit

Most holy Virgin Immaculate, my Mother Mary, it is to you, who are the Mother of my Lord, the Queen of the world, the advocate, the hope and the refuge of sinners, that I have recourse today, I, who most of all am deserving of pity. Most humbly do I offer you my homage, O great Queen, and I thank you for all the graces you have obtained for me until now, and particularly for having saved me from Hell, which, by my sins, I have so often deserved.

I love you, O most lovable Lady, and because of my love for you, I promise to serve you always and to do all in my power to win others to love you also. In your hands I place all my hopes; I entrust the salvation of my soul to your care. Accept me as your servant, O Mother of Mercy; receive me under your mantle. And since you have such power with God, deliver me from all temptations, or rather, obtain for me the strength to triumph over them until death. Of you I ask the grace of a perfect love for Jesus Christ. Through your help I hope to die a happy death. O my Mother, I beg you, by the love you bear to God, to help me at all times, but especially at the last moment of my life. Do not leave me, I beseech you, until you see me safe in Heaven, blessing you and singing your mercies for all eternity.

Amen, so I hope, so may it be.

First Visit

PRAYER: "MY LORD JESUS CHRIST . . ." (page 1).

JESUS in the Blessed Sacrament is the source of everything that is good. He says to us: *If any man thirst, let him come to Me, and drink.* (*John* 7:37). What torrents of grace have not the saints drawn from the fountain of the Blessed Sacrament! For it is there that Jesus distributes all the merits of His passion, as the Prophet Isaias foretold: *You shall draw waters with joy out of the Saviour's fountains.* (*Is.* 12:3). The Countess of Feria, who afterwards became a Poor Clare, was called the spouse of the Blessed Sacrament because of her long and frequent visits to It. When she was asked how she spent the many hours passed in this way in the presence of the Holy of Holies, she replied: "I could remain there for eternity. For is there not present there the very essence of God, which will be the food of the blessed in Heaven? And do you ask me what I do in His presence? Why not rather ask what is *not* done there?

I love Him, I praise and thank Him and I ask for favors. What does a poor man do in the presence of a rich man? What does a sick man do in the presence of his doctor? What does a man parched with thirst do when he comes to a clear fountain? What does a starving man do when put sitting before a well-supplied table?"

O my most sweet and beloved Jesus, You who are my life, my hope, my treasure and the only love of my heart, what has it not cost You to remain with us in the Blessed Sacrament! So as to be able to dwell among us on our altars, You had to die; and in order to help us by Your presence there, how many insults have You not had to endure since then! Your love for us, and the desire You have that we should love You, have outweighed everything.

Come then, O Lord, come into my heart! Close its doors forever so that for the future no creature may enter it to share the love which is due to You, that love which I desire to bestow entirely on You. Do You alone, my dear Redeemer, rule me; do You alone possess my whole being. And if ever I do not obey You perfectly, punish me severely, that I may be more careful to please You for the future. Grant that I may never again seek any pleasure other than that of pleasing You, of visiting You often, of speaking with You and of receiving You in Holy Communion. Let all who wish for other treasures seek them; the only treasure I love, the only one I desire, is that of Your love. It is for that alone I ask at the foot of the altar. Make me forget myself, so that I may remember only Your goodness. Blessed Seraphim, I envy you, not for your glory, but for the love you have for your God and mine. Teach me what I must do to love Him and to please Him.

Aspiration: My Jesus, I will love only You; You are the only one I wish to please.

SPIRITUAL COMMUNION (page 2).

Visit To Our Lady

Our Mother Mary is another fountain from which we can also draw the waters of grace. As St. Bernard says, she is so rich in favors and graces that there is no one in the world who does not share in them. The Angel greeted her with the words: "Hail! full of grace!" The Blessed Virgin was filled with grace by God that she might afterwards give it to all who are devout to her.

Aspiration: Cause of our joy, pray for us!

PRAYER: "MOST HOLY VIRGIN . . ." (page 3).

Second Visit

PRAYER: "MY LORD JESUS CHRIST . . ." (page 1).

THE devout Father Nieremberg says that since bread is a food which is consumed by eating and which keeps when preserved, Jesus wished to dwell on earth under its species, not only to be consumed by uniting Himself in Holy Communion to souls that love Him, but also to be preserved in the Tabernacle so as to be present with us and, in this way, remind us of the love He has for us. St. Paul says: *He emptied Himself, taking the form of a servant. (Phil.* 2:7). But what must we say when we see Him taking the form of bread? "The greatness of the love which Jesus has for every soul in the state of grace," says St. Peter of Alcantara, "is something that no tongue could adequately express. When He wished to depart this life, this sweet Spouse of souls, lest His absence might cause them to forget Him, left to them as a memorial the Blessed Sacrament, in which He Himself remained. His own self was the only pledge He wished should remain between these souls and Himself, that they might always remember Him."

Since, then, my Jesus, You are enclosed in this Tabernacle to receive the petitions of poor creatures who come to visit You, listen today to the petition of the most ungrateful sinner on earth.

I come repentant to Your feet, for I am well aware of the evil I have done in displeasing You. My first prayer is that You will pardon all my sins. Ah, my God, would that I had never offended You! After that, I must tell You my next desire. Now that I have found out how infinitely good You are, I have been drawn to love You. I feel an ardent desire to love You and to please You, but I have not the strength to give effect to that desire unless You help me. O great Lord, show to the whole court of Heaven Your immense goodness and Your supreme power. Change me from the great rebel I have been up to the present into one who loves You very much. You have the power to do so, and I know it is Your wish. Make up for all that is wanting in me, that

thus I may be able to love You very much—
at least that I may love You as much as I
have offended You. I love You, my Jesus,
above all things; I love You more than my
life, O my God, my Love, my All!
Aspiration: My God and my All!

SPIRITUAL COMMUNION (page 2).

Visit To Our Lady

*Let us go therefore with confidence to the
throne of grace, that we may obtain mercy,
and find grace in seasonable aid.* (*Heb.*
4:16).

St. Antoninus tells us that this throne,
from which God distributes all graces, is
Our Blessed Lady. O most lovable Queen,
since you are so very anxious to help sinners, see here a great sinner who has
recourse to you. Help me very much, and
help me without delay!
Aspiration: Sole refuge of sinners, have pity
on me!

PRAYER: "MOST HOLY VIRGIN . . ." (page 3).

Third Visit

PRAYER: "MY LORD JESUS CHRIST . . ." (page 1).

My delights were to be with the children of men. (Prov. 8:31).

HERE is our Jesus saying to us that He takes delight in the company of men—our Jesus, who was not satisfied with dying for love of us when He was on earth, but wished to remain with us, even after His death, in the Blessed Sacrament. "O men," St. Teresa cries out, "how can you offend a God who says that it is in your company He takes delight!" Jesus takes His delight in our company. Shall not we take ours in His, we especially who have had the honor to be welcomed into His palace? Certainly those subjects whom a king allows to enter his own palace consider themselves very greatly honored. Here is the palace of our King—here where we now are with Jesus Christ. Let us learn to thank Him for the privilege and avail ourselves of His company to talk to Him.

O my Lord and my God, I am here before

this altar on which You remain night and day for my sake. You are the source of everything that is good; You are the healer of illness of every kind; You are the wealth of everyone who is poor. See now at Your feet a sinner who asks Your mercy, one who is, of all sinners, the poorest and most seriously ill. Have pity on me! Now that I see how, in the Blessed Sacrament, You have come down from Heaven upon earth for the sole purpose of doing good to me, I shall not lose heart at the sight of my wretchedness. I praise You, I thank You, I love You. And if You wish that I should ask You for a favor, this is what I ask: oh, listen to me! I wish never to offend You again, and that You give me light and grace to love You with all my strength. O my Lord, I love You with all my heart and soul. Grant that when I say this it may be really true and that I may say it always—in this life, and for eternity. Mary most holy, my holy patrons, you Angels and Saints of Paradise, help me to love my God, who is so worthy of love.

Aspiration: O Good Shepherd, true Bread, Jesus, have mercy on us. Feed us, guard us, grant us happiness in life eternal.

Spiritual Communion (page 2).

Visit To Our Lady

Her bands are a healthful binding. (*Ecclus.* 6:31).

Pelbart tells us that devotion to Mary is an assurance of salvation for us. Let us ask our Queen to bind us ever more closely to herself by teaching us to love her and to have confidence in her protection.

Aspiration: O clement, O loving, O sweet Virgin Mary!

Prayer: "Most Holy Virgin . . ." (page 3).

Fourth Visit

Prayer: "My Lord Jesus Christ . . ." (page 1).

Her conversation hath no bitterness, nor her company any tediousness. (*Wis.* 8:16).

PEOPLE who are friends are so happy in being together that they can spend whole days in one another's company without growing tired. In the case of Jesus in the Blessed Sacrament, our Friend, it is only those who do not love Him who grow weary in His presence. After her death, St. Teresa [of Avila], who was already in Heaven, said to one of her nuns: "There should be no difference, as far as purity and love are concerned, between the blessed in Heaven and the faithful on earth, though we are perfectly happy and you are suffering. What the Divine Essence is to us in Heaven, the Blessed Sacrament should be to you on earth." Here, then, is our Heaven on earth—the Most Blessed Sacrament.

O Immaculate Lamb, sacrificed on the Cross for us, remember that I am one of those souls You have redeemed by Your death and at the cost of so much suffering. Since You have given Yourself to me, and continue to do so every day by sacrificing Yourself on the altar because of Your love for me, grant that I may belong completely to You and that I may nevermore lose You. I give myself entirely to You, to do with me what You wish. I give You my will. Chain it with the sweet bonds of Your love, that it may always be the slave of Your holy will. I have no longer any wish to live for the satisfaction of my desires. My only wish is to please You. Destroy in me everything that does not please You. Grant me the grace never to have any other thought than to please You, any other desire than what You desire. I love You, my dear Saviour, with my whole heart. I love You because You desire that I should love You. I love You because You really deserve my love. I am very sorry that I do not love You as much as You deserve. I desire, O Lord, to die for love of You. Accept my desire, and give me Your love.

Aspiration: I sacrifice myself entirely to the good pleasure of God.

SPIRITUAL COMMUNION (page 2).

Visit To Our Lady

Mary says: *I am the mother of fair love* (*Ecclus.* 24:24), that is, of the love which makes souls beautiful. St. Mary Magdalen of Pazzi saw Mary going about dispensing divine love as a sweet liquid. Mary is the only one who dispenses this gift; from her let us seek it.

Aspiration: My Mother, my hope, make me belong entirely to Jesus.

PRAYER: "MOST HOLY VIRGIN . . ." (page 3).

Fifth Visit

PRAYER: "MY LORD JESUS CHRIST . . ." (page 1).

The sparrow hath found herself a house, and the turtledove a nest for herself where she may lay her young ones: Thy altars, O Lord of hosts, my King and my God. (Ps. 83:4).

THE sparrow and the turtledove, says David, make a home for themselves in their nests; but it is on the altar that You, my King and my God, have found a home and a nest for Yourself, that You might live in our midst and that we might be able to find You there always.

Lord, we cannot help saying that You love men too much. You do not know what more You can do to win their love. O my beloved Jesus, give us the grace to love You in turn with our whole heart. It is not just that our love for a God who loves us as tenderly as You should be cold or lukewarm. Draw us to Yourself by the sweet attraction of

Your love. Make us realize the claim You have on all the love of our hearts.

O Infinite Majesty and Infinite Goodness, You love men so much, You have done so much that men might love You, yet how is it that among men there are so few who really love You? No longer will I be as I have been up to the present—one of those ungrateful ones. I am determined to love You as much as I can, and to love none other but You. You deserve it; and, so forcefully do You even command me to do so, that I am resolved to satisfy You. Grant, O my God, that I may satisfy You fully. By the merits of Your Passion I beg of You to grant me this favor, and from the same merits I confidently hope for it. Bestow the goods of the earth on those who desire them. The only treasure I seek and desire is the great treasure of Your love. I love You, my Jesus; I love You, Infinite Goodness. You are all my wealth, all my happiness, all my love.

Aspiration: My Jesus, You have given Yourself entirely to me. I give myself entirely to You.

SPIRITUAL COMMUNION (page 2).

Visit To Our Lady

My Lady, St. Bernard calls you the ravisher of hearts. He says that you go about stealing hearts by the charms of your beauty and goodness. Steal, I beseech you, my heart and will, too. I give them entirely to you. Offer them to God with your own. *Aspiration:* Mother most amiable, pray for me!

PRAYER: "MOST HOLY VIRGIN . . ." (page 3).

Sixth Visit

PRAYER: "MY LORD JESUS CHRIST . . ." (page 1).

Where your treasure is, there will your heart be also. (Luke 12:34).

JESUS CHRIST says that a person centers his affection in what he considers to be his treasure, wherever it may be. And therefore the Saints, who consider Jesus Christ to be their only treasure, center all the love of their hearts in the Blessed Sacrament.

My most beloved Jesus, hidden under the sacramental veils, it is because of Your love for me that You remain night and day enclosed in this Tabernacle. Draw, I beg of You, my whole heart to Yourself, that I may think of no one else but You, that I may love and confide in You alone. By the merits of Your Passion, I ask You for this favor, and through them I hope to obtain it.

Ah, my sacramental Saviour and divine Lover, how full of kindness and tenderness are the means Your love has invented to win the love of souls! O Eternal Word, You were not satisfied with becoming man and dying for us. You have also given us the Blessed Sacrament as a companion, as food, and as a guarantee of Heaven. At one time You show Yourself to us as an infant in a stable, at another as a poor man in a workshop, then as a criminal on a cross, and now as bread on an altar. Tell me, could You invent any other means to win our love? O Infinite Goodness, when shall I really begin to correspond with such a refinement of love? Lord, I wish to live for the one purpose of loving You alone. And of what use is life to me if I do not spend it entirely in loving and pleasing You, my beloved Redeemer, Who have spent Your whole life for me? And what have I to love if not You, Who are all beauty, all condescension, all goodness, all loving, all worthy of love? May I live only to love You. May the mere remembrance of Your love melt my heart with love. May the very words *Crib* and *Cross* and *Sacrament* inflame it with the desire to do great things for You, O my Jesus, Who have indeed done so much and suffered so greatly for me. *Aspiration:* Grant, my Lord, that before I die I may do something for You!

SPIRITUAL COMMUNION (page 2).

Visit To Our Lady

As a fair olive tree in the plains. (*Ecclus.* 24:19).

I am this beautiful olive tree, says Mary, from which the oil of mercy is always flowing. And I am standing in the plain so that everyone may see me and may have recourse to me. Let us say with St. Bernard: Remember, O most compassionate Mary, that you have never been known at any time to abandon anyone who had recourse to your protection.

Aspiration: O Mary, grant me the grace to have recourse to you always.

PRAYER: "MOST HOLY VIRGIN . . ." (page 3).

Seventh Visit

PRAYER: "MY LORD JESUS CHRIST . . ." (page 1).

Behold I am with you all days, even to the consummation of the world. (Matt. 28:20).

OUR loving Shepherd, who has given His life for us who are His sheep, would not separate Himself from us by death. My beloved sheep, He says, I am always with you. It is for you I have remained on earth in this Sacrament; here you find Me whenever you wish, ready to help and console you by My presence. As long as you are on earth I shall not leave you.

The Bridegroom, says St. Peter of Alcantara, wished to leave His bride a companion so that she might not be alone during His long absence; and so He left this Sacrament in which He Himself, the best companion He could leave her, remains.

My dearest Lord, my most amiable Saviour, I am now visiting You on this altar. But You return me the visit with much greater love when You come into my soul in Holy Communion. You are then not only present to me, but You become my food, giving and uniting Yourself completely to me, so that I can then say with truth: My Jesus, You are now all mine.

Since, then, You give Yourself entirely to me, it is only reasonable that I should give myself entirely to You. I am a worm, and You are God. O God of love, O Love of my heart, when shall I find that I belong entirely to You in deed, and not in word only? You have the power to bring this about. By the merits of Your Precious Blood, increase my trust in You, so that I may be confident of obtaining from You before I die the grace to belong wholly to You and to be my own in nothing at all. O Lord, You hear the prayers of everyone; hear now the prayer of a soul that desires really to love You. I wish to love You with all my strength. I desire to obey You in everything that You wish, without self-interest, without consolation, without reward. I wish to serve You out of love, only to please You, only to content Your Heart, which loves me so very dearly. To love You will be my reward. O beloved Son of the Eternal Father, take possession of my liberty, of my will, of all that I possess, of my whole self, and give me Yourself. I love You, I long for You, I desire You.

Aspiration: My Jesus, make me all Your own.

SPIRITUAL COMMUNION (page 2).

Visit To Our Lady

Our own most loving Lady, the whole Church declares you to be our hope and salutes you under that title. Since you are the hope of us all, be my hope too. St. Bernard called you the whole foundation of his hope and said: Let him who is in despair, hope in Mary. And so will I too address you: My own Mary, you save even those who are in despair; in you I place all my hope.

Aspiration: Mary, Mother of God, pray to Jesus for me.

PRAYER: "MOST HOLY VIRGIN . . ." (page 3).

Eighth Visit

PRAYER: "MY LORD JESUS CHRIST . . . (page 1).

TO everyone who visits Him in the Blessed Sacrament Jesus addresses the words He said to the spouse in the Canticles: *Arise, make haste, my love, my dove, my beautiful one, and come. (Cant.* 2:10). You that are now visiting Me, *arise* from your misery; I am here to enrich you with graces. *Make haste* to come near to Me; do not be afraid of My majesty, for it has hidden itself in this Sacrament to take away your fear and to give you confidence. *My beloved*—since you love Me and I love you, you are no longer My enemy but My friend. *My beautiful one*—My grace has made you beautiful. *And come,* draw near, and throw yourself into My arms, and ask Me with the greatest confidence for whatever you wish.

St. Teresa says that the King of Glory has concealed His majesty under the appearance of bread in the Blessed Sacrament to encourage us to approach His Divine Heart with greater confidence. Let us, then, draw near to Jesus with great confidence and love; let us unite ourselves to Him and ask Him for graces.

O Eternal Word made man and present for my sake in the Blessed Sacrament, what joy should be mine now that I am in the presence of my God, who is infinitely good and has so tender a love for me! O you souls that love God, whether you be in Heaven or on earth, love Him for me also. Mary, my Mother, help me to love Him.

And I ask You, dear Lord, to make Yourself the object of all my love. Make Yourself complete Master of my will. Take full possession of me. To You I consecrate my mind, that it may always think of Your Goodness; I consecrate my body to You, that it may help me to please You; I consecrate to You my soul, that it may belong entirely to You. Would, O God, that all men knew the tenderness of Your love for them, that they might live only to honor and please You, as You wish and deserve. May I, at least, always love You. From this day forward I wish to do all I can to please You. I am determined to do everything that I know to be pleasing to You, even though it would cost me great suffering and the loss of everything, even of life itself. Fortunate shall I be if I lose everything to gain You,

my God, my Treasure, my Love, my All!
Aspiration: Jesus, my Love, take all that I
have; take complete possession of me.

SPIRITUAL COMMUNION (page 2).

Visit To Our Lady

*Whosoever is a little one, let him come to
me.* (*Prov.* 9:4). Mary invites all who need
a mother to go to her, as they would to the
most loving of mothers. Fr. Nieremberg tells
us that the love of all mothers together is
but a shadow compared to the love Mary
has for each one of us. O Mary, Mother of
my soul, you who love me and desire my
salvation more than anyone else after God,
show yourself a mother.
Aspiration: My Mother, grant that I may
always remember you.

PRAYER: "MOST HOLY VIRGIN . . ." (page 3).

Ninth Visit

PRAYER: "MY LORD JESUS CHRIST . . ." (page 1).

THE Venerable Father Alvarez saw Jesus in the Blessed Sacrament with His hands filled with graces, seeking to whom He might distribute them. St. Catherine of Siena is said to have approached the Most Holy Sacrament with the loving eagerness of a child turning to its mother's breast.

O most beloved only-begotten Son of the Eternal Father, I know that You, more than all else, deserve to be loved very much. I desire to love You as much as You deserve, or at least as much as a soul can ever wish to love You. I fully realize that, since I have rebelled against Your love and betrayed it, I do not deserve to love You, nor do I deserve to come as near to You as I now am in this church. But still, in spite of that, I feel that You are longing for my love. I hear You say: *My child, give Me your heart. You shall love the Lord your God with your whole heart.* I know that You have spared my life and not sent me to Hell so that I may one day give my heart completely to loving You. Since, then, You desire to be loved even by me, O my God, I am ready. I surrender myself to You; I give myself to You. O God, Who are all goodness, all love, I love You. I choose You as the only king and lord of my poor heart. You wish to possess that heart, and I wish to give it to You. It is cold, it is loathsome. But if you accept it, You will change it. Change me, my Lord, change me. I cannot any longer bear to live as I have done up to the present—ungrateful, and with so little love for that infinite goodness of Yours which loves me so much and deserves so much love. For the future, help me to compensate You for all the love I have neglected to give You in the past.

Aspiration: My God, my God, I wish to love You. I wish to love You.

SPIRITUAL COMMUNION (page 2).

Visit To Our Lady

Mary, the Mother of Jesus, is like her Son in everything. As she is the Mother of Mercy, it is her delight to help and console the miserable. So greatly does this Mother desire to grant graces to everyone that

Bernardine de Bustis says: "Far greater is her desire to do good and to impart grace to you than your desire to receive it."
Aspiration: Hail our hope!

PRAYER: "MOST HOLY VIRGIN . . ." (page 3).

Tenth Visit

PRAYER: "MY LORD JESUS CHRIST . . ." (page 1).

O YOU foolish, worldly minded creatures, says St. Augustine, unhappy that you are, where are you seeking satisfaction for the longing of your hearts? Come to Jesus, for He is the only one who can bestow on you that happiness you are seeking.

My soul, do not be so foolish; seek only God: seek the one Good which includes in Itself everything that is good. And if you desire to find Him immediately, see—He is quite close to you. Tell Him what you desire, for it is to console you and grant your prayer that He remains in the Tabernacle. St. Teresa says that it is not everyone that is allowed to speak directly to his king. The most one can hope for is to communicate with him through a third person. But to talk with You, O King of Glory, there is no need for a third person. In the Sacrament of the Altar You are always ready to give audience to everyone. Whoever wishes can always find You there and may speak with you face to face. And even if anyone should at last succeed in speaking with a king, how many difficulties has he not had to surmount before doing so! Kings grant audiences only a few times in the year, but in this Sacrament, You, Who are our King, grant audience to all, night and day, and at any time we please.

O Sacrament of Love, whether You give Yourself in Holy Communion or dwell on the altar, You know how to draw countless hearts to Yourself by the tender attraction of Your love. Drawn by love for You, and astonished at such goodness on Your part, they burn with joy and always think of You. Draw also my poor heart to You, since it desires to love You and to live as the slave of Your love. For my part, from this day forward, I place in Your hands all my interests, all my hope for the future, my affection, my soul, my body—everything. Accept me, O Lord, and do with me whatever pleases You. I will never again complain, O my Love, of Your holy designs. I know that since they all proceed from Your loving Heart they will be full of love, and for my good. It is enough for me to know that You will them; I also will them, in time and in eternity. Do all that You will in me and with me. I unite myself entirely to Your will, which is all holy, all good, all perfect and all lovable. O Will of my God, how dear are You to me! All during my life, and at my death, it is my wish to be united to You. Your pleasure is my pleasure; may Your will be also my will! My God, my God, help me. Grant that for the future I may live only for You, only to do Your will and to love doing it. Since You have died for me and become my food, may I die for love of You. I curse those days in which, to Your great displeasure, I followed my own will. O Will of God, I love You as much as I love God, since You are one with Him. I love You with my whole heart and give myself entirely to You.

Aspiration: O Will of God, You are my love.

SPIRITUAL COMMUNION (page 2).

Visit To Our Lady

Mary, our Queen, says, *"With me are riches . . . that I may enrich them that love me."* (*Prov.* 8:18, 21). If we wish to be rich in graces, let us love Mary. Raymund Jordanus calls her the treasurer of graces. Blessed is he who has recourse to Mary with love and confidence. My Mother, my hope, it is in your power to make me a saint; I hope for this favor from you.
Aspiration: Mother most amiable, pray for me.

PRAYER: "MOST HOLY VIRGIN . . ." (page 3).

Eleventh Visit

PRAYER: "MY LORD JESUS CHRIST . . ." (page 1).

LET us be careful, says St. Teresa, not to go far away from Jesus, our beloved Shepherd, nor to lose sight of Him; because the sheep that remain near their shepherd are more favored and receive more fondling than the others, and he always gives them some choice part of what he himself is eating. If the shepherd should happen to sleep, the sheep who still remain near him, and either awaken him or wait until he wakens, are fondled anew and receive new favors.

My Sacramental Redeemer, I am now near to You, Who are my Shepherd. The only favor I ask of You is to love You with fervor and to persevere in that love.

O holy Faith, I thank you for teaching and assuring me that in the divine Sacrament of the Altar, in that *heavenly* bread, *bread* does not exist; but rather, that in it my Lord Jesus Christ is really and entirely present and that He is present there because He loves me. My Lord and my All, I believe that You are present in the Most Holy Sacrament. Though eyes of flesh and blood cannot see You, by the light of holy Faith I discern You in the consecrated Host as King of Heaven and earth and as the Saviour of the world.

My most sweet Jesus, as You are the source of my hope and my salvation, of my strength and consolation, I wish too that You should be the object of all my thoughts and desires, of all my love. I take more delight in the perfect happiness You have, and will ever have, in Yourself, than in any good that could ever come to me in time or in eternity. My greatest joy is that You, my beloved Redeemer, are perfectly happy and that Your happiness is infinite. Reign, my Lord, over my whole heart; I give it all to You: take possession of it forever. May my will, my senses and my faculties all be directed to loving You, and as long as I live, may they never serve for anything else than to give You satisfaction and glory.

A life such as this was yours, O Mary most holy, Mother and first lover of my Jesus. I ask that you help me, that you obtain for me, for the future, the happiness of living as you always did—for God alone. *Aspiration:* My Jesus, may I be all Yours, and may You be all mine.

SPIRITUAL COMMUNION (page 2).

Visit To Our Lady

Blessed is the man . . . that watcheth daily at my gates, and waiteth at the posts of my doors. (*Prov.* 8:34). Blessed is he who, like the poor who beg alms at the gates of the rich, seeks the alms of graces at the doors of the mercy of Mary! And more blessed still is he who strives to imitate the virtues he sees in Mary, especially her purity and humility.

Aspiration: My hope, help me!

PRAYER: "MOST HOLY VIRGIN . . ." (page 3).

Twelfth Visit

PRAYER: "MY LORD JESUS CHRIST . . ." (page 1).

God is charity, and he that abideth in charity, abideth in God, and God in him. (1 John 4:16).

THE person who loves Jesus lives in His company, and Jesus lives in his. *If any one love Me . . . My Father will love him and We will come to him, and will make Our abode with him. (John 14:23).* When St. Philip Neri saw the Blessed Sacrament, which was being brought to him as Viaticum, enter his room, he cried out: "Behold my Love! Behold my Love!" And here, where Jesus is present in the Blessed Sacrament, let each one of us, too, say: "Behold my Love! Here is the object of my entire love through my whole life and through eternity."

My Lord and my God, since You have said in the Gospel that You will love the man who loves You, and that You will come to dwell in him and never leave him, I love You more than anything else that is good. I beg that You, too, love me, for I set greater store by your love for me than by all the kingdoms of the world. Come and live in the poor dwelling of my heart in such a way that You may never leave me, or rather, that I may never drive You away. It is only when You are driven that You go away. But as I have done this in the past, I might easily do it again. Ah, do not allow such a new act of wickedness and horrible ingratitude to happen that I, whom You have so specially favored and on whom You have showered so many graces, should drive You from my soul! Still, this might happen. And so, my Lord, I desire to die, if it pleases You, so that by dying when united to You, I may live united to You forever. Yes, O my Jesus, for this I hope. I embrace You and press You to my poor heart. Grant that I may always love You and always be loved by You. You will always love me. I trust that we shall always love each other, O my God, throughout eternity.

Aspiration: My Jesus, I wish always to love You and be loved by You.

SPIRITUAL COMMUNION (page 2).

Visit To Our Lady

They that work by me shall not sin. They that explain me shall have life everlasting. (Ecclus. 24:30, 31). Mary says that whoever strives to honor her shall persevere in grace to the end. And those who make her known and loved by others will be numbered among the elect. Promise that whenever you can, in public or in private, you will speak of the glories of Mary and of devotion to her.

Aspiration: Grant that I may praise you, O holy Virgin!

PRAYER: "MOST HOLY VIRGIN . . ." (page 3).

Thirteenth Visit

PRAYER: "MY LORD JESUS CHRIST . . ." (page 1).

My eyes and my heart shall be there always. (3 Kgs. 9:3).

JESUS has fulfilled this beautiful promise in the Sacrament of the Altar, where He lives with us night and day. My Lord, would it not have been enough for You to remain in the Blessed Sacrament during the day only, when You could have someone to adore You and keep You company? Why remain the whole night as well, when all the churches are closed and men retire to their homes, leaving You quite alone? But I understand You. It is love that has made You our prisoner. It is the very great love You have for us that has kept You on earth, unable to leave us either night or day.

Ah, my loving Saviour, this very great love of Yours should, of itself, make all men ever stay near You in the sacred ciboria unless they be driven away by force! And when they do go, they should leave at the foot of the altar their hearts filled with love for God Incarnate who remains alone and hidden in a Tabernacle—for a God who is ever alert to see our needs and to provide for them, who is all heart to love us and who longs for the coming day that He may be visited again by those He loves.

Yes, my Jesus, I wish to please You. I consecrate my will and all my love entirely to You. O Infinite Majesty of God, You have left Yourself in this Sacrament not only to be near us and with us, but especially to give Yourself to souls, souls that You love so much. But, Lord, who will presume to approach You to eat Your flesh? But who, on the other hand, can keep at a distance from You? It is precisely that You might be able to enter into us and take possession of our hearts that You hide Yourself in the consecrated Host. You long that we should receive You and are delighted to be united to our hearts. Come, then, my Jesus, come! I desire to receive You within me, that You may be the God of my heart and of my will. All that is in me I yield, my dear Redeemer, to Your love. Satisfaction, pleasure, self-will—all I give to You. O God of Love, conquer me entirely and rule over me. Destroy in me everything that is merely mine and does not belong to You. Do not permit, O

my Love, that my soul, which is filled with
the majesty of God when it receives You in
Holy Communion, should attach itself again
to creatures. I love You, my God, I love You,
and I will love You only, and that always.
Aspiration: Draw me by the chains of Your
love.

SPIRITUAL COMMUNION (page 2).

Visit To Our Lady

St. Bernard thus exhorts us: "Let us seek
for grace, and let us seek it through Mary."
She is the treasury of divine graces. It is
in her power to enrich us, and she wishes
to do so. And so she invites us and calls to
us: *Whosoever is a little one, let him come
to me.* (*Prov.* 9:4). Most loving Lady, most
gracious and exalted Lady, look on a poor
sinner who recommends himself to you and
who places all his confidence in you.
Aspiration: We fly to your patronage, O holy
Mother of God.

PRAYER: "MOST HOLY VIRGIN . . ." (page 3).

Fourteenth Visit

PRAYER: "MY LORD JESUS CHRIST . . ." (page 1).

MOST loving Jesus, I hear You say from the Tabernacle where You are present: *This is My rest for ever and ever: here will I dwell, for I have chosen it.* (Ps. 131:14). Since You have chosen to dwell among us, remaining on the altar in the Blessed Sacrament, and because it is Your love for us that makes You find Your rest there, it is only just that our hearts, too, should dwell with You in their love, and should find in You all their rest and joy. Happy are you, O loving souls, who can find no sweeter rest in all the world than in remaining near to your Sacramental Jesus! And happy should I be, my Lord, were it for the future to be my greatest joy to remain always in Your presence, or always to think of You, Who, in the Blessed Sacrament, are always thinking of me and of my welfare.

Ah, my Lord, why have I lost so many years in which I have not loved You? I curse those unhappy years, and I bless the infinite patience of God for having borne with me for so long, ungrateful though I have been. And yet, in spite of this ingratitude, You are still waiting for me. And why, my God, why? So that one day, conquered by Your mercy and Your love, I may surrender myself completely to You. Lord, I will no longer resist. I will no longer be ungrateful. It is only just that I should consecrate to You at least the time I have still to live, whether it be long or short. O my Jesus, I hope that You will help me to belong entirely to You. You were so good to me when I fled from You and despised Your love that I have the firmest hope that You will help me even more now, when I am seeking You and really wish to love You. O my God, worthy of infinite love, give me, then, the grace to love You. I love You with my whole heart. I love You above everything. I love You more than myself, more than my life. I am sorry for having offended You, O Infinite Goodness; pardon me, and with Your pardon, grant me the grace to love You very much in this life and forever in the next. O omnipotent God, show Your power to the world by making one who has been as ungrateful as I to be one of Your greatest lovers. Do this by Your merits, O my Jesus. I wish to love You thus my whole life long; I beseech You, Who place this wish in my heart, strengthen me.

Aspiration: My Jesus, I thank You for having waited for me until now.

SPIRITUAL COMMUNION (page 2).

Visit To Our Lady

St. Germanus, speaking to Mary, says: "No one is saved but through you; no one is delivered from evil but through you; no one receives any grace but through you." And so, O Lady who are my hope, if you do not help me, I am lost and shall be unable to come and bless you in Heaven. But, O Lady, I hear all the Saints say that you do not abandon those who have recourse to you. Only he who has not recourse to you is lost. Miserable as I am, I have recourse to you and place all my hope in you.

Aspiration: All my confidence is in Mary; she is the ground of all my hope.

PRAYER: "MOST HOLY VIRGIN . . ." (page 3).

Fifteenth Visit

PRAYER: "MY LORD JESUS CHRIST . . ." (page 1).

I am come to cast fire on the earth: and what will I, but that it be kindled? (Luke 12:49).

FRANCIS Olimpio, the Theatine, said that nothing on earth enkindled so ardent a fire of divine love in the hearts of men as the Blessed Sacrament of the Altar. To St. Catherine of Siena, Our Lord in the Blessed Sacrament revealed Himself as a furnace of love from which flames poured forth over the whole earth. The Saint was astonished that men could live without burning with love for God, seeing how much He loved them. My Jesus, make me burn with love for You; grant that all my thoughts and desires may be for You only. Happy should I be were this holy fire of Your love to take complete possession of my heart, and, as I advance in years, gradually to consume in me all love for earthly things.

O Divine Word, O my Jesus, I see You sacrificed and immolated on the altar for love of me. Since You sacrifice Yourself as a victim of love for me, I should consecrate myself entirely to You. Yes, my God and my King, this day I consecrate entirely to You my soul, my self, my will and all my life. O Eternal Father, I unite this sacrifice of mine, so poor in itself, to that sacrifice of infinite worth which Jesus, Your Son and my Saviour, once offered on the cross to You, and still offers on our altars so many times every day. Through the merits of Jesus, accept it, and grant me the grace to renew it every day of my life, and, in dying, to sacrifice myself entirely to Your glory. I long for the grace granted to so many martyrs, to die for love of You. But if I am unworthy of so great a grace as that, grant me at least, my Lord, to sacrifice my life to You by accepting the death You will send me. O Lord, I desire this grace. I wish to have the intention of honoring and pleasing You in the death I die. From this moment I sacrifice my life to You, and I offer You my death, when and wherever it may take place.

Aspiration: My Jesus, I wish that my death may be an act of submission pleasing to You!

SPIRITUAL COMMUNION (page 2).

Visit To Our Lady

Allow me, too, my most sweet Queen, to call you, with your own St. Bernard, the whole ground of my hope, and to say with St. John Damascene that I have placed all my hope in you. You must obtain for me the forgiveness of my sins, perseverance until death and deliverance from Purgatory. It is through you that all who are saved obtain their salvation. And so, O Mary, it is you who must save me. He whom you wish to be saved, will be saved. Only wish my salvation, and I shall be saved. You save all those who call on you. I am now calling on you and say to you:

Aspiration: O salvation of those who call on you, save me!

PRAYER: "MOST HOLY VIRGIN . . ." (page 3).

Sixteenth Visit

PRAYER: "MY LORD JESUS CHRIST . . ." (page 1).

IF men always had recourse to the Blessed Sacrament to find there a remedy for all their troubles, they certainly would not be as unhappy as they are. *Is there no balm in Galaad or is there no physician there?* laments Jeremias. (8:22). Galaad in Arabia, a mountain that produces fragrant ointments, is a figure of Jesus Christ, who, in this Sacrament, has provided all the remedies for our afflictions. Why, then, O children of Adam, our Redeemer seems to ask, do you complain of your misfortunes when you have, in the Blessed Sacrament, the physician and the remedy for them all? *Come to me . . . and I will refresh you. (Matt.* 11:28). I wish, then, O Lord, to say to You with the sisters of Lazarus: *Lord, behold, he whom Thou lovest is sick. (John* 11:3).

Lord, I am that unhappy sinner You love. My soul is wounded by the sins I have committed; I come to You, my Divine Physician, that You may cure me. You have the power and the will to do so: *Heal my soul, for I have sinned against Thee. (Ps. 40:5).*

Draw me completely to Yourself, my most sweet Jesus, by the all-winning attraction of Your love. I would rather be united to You than be made ruler of the whole earth. I desire nothing else in the world but to love You. I have but little to give You; yet, if I could gain possession of all the kingdoms of the earth, I would do so, that I might renounce them all again for love of You. For Your sake, then, I renounce what I can—all relatives, comforts and pleasures, even spiritual consolation. For Your sake I renounce my liberty and my will. It is on You I wish to bestow all my love. I love You, Infinite Goodness. I love You more than myself, and I hope to love You forever.

Aspiration: My Jesus, I give myself to You. In pity, accept me, I beg You.

SPIRITUAL COMMUNION (page 2).

Visit To Our Lady

My Lady, you said to St. Bridget: "However much a man sins, if he returns to me with a real purpose of amendment, I am instantly ready to receive him; I do not consider the number of his sins, but only the dispositions with which he comes. I do not disdain to anoint and heal his wounds, for I am called, and really am, the Mother of Mercy." Since, then, O heavenly physician, you have both the power and the desire to heal me, I have recourse to you. Heal the many wounds of my soul. If you say but a single word to your Son on my behalf, I shall be cured.

Aspiration: O Mary, have pity on me!

PRAYER: "MOST HOLY VIRGIN . . ." (page 3).

Seventeenth Visit

PRAYER: "MY LORD JESUS CHRIST . . ." (page 1).

FOR those who are in love there is no greater pleasure than to be in one another's company. If we, then, are much in love with Jesus Christ, we are now in His presence, and what a pleasure that should be for us! Jesus in the Blessed Sacrament sees us and hears us. Have we nothing to say to Him? Let us console ourselves in His company; let us take delight in His glory and in the love that so many souls have for the Blessed Sacrament. Let it be our desire that everyone should love Jesus in the Tabernacle and consecrate their hearts to Him. Let us, at least, consecrate entirely to Him our love. Father Salès, of the Society of Jesus, derived happiness merely from speaking of the Most Blessed Sacrament, and he could never visit It often enough. Whenever he went about the house, was called to the parlor or was returning to his room, he took occasion to visit his beloved Lord, so much so that it was remarked that he allowed scarcely an hour of the day to pass without visiting Him. Later on, he obtained the favor of dying at the hands of heretics while defending the truth of the Real Presence.

Would that I, too, O most loving Jesus, had the happiness of dying for so noble a cause as the defense of this Sacrament, by means of which You have taught us how tender is the love You have for us. And since, my Lord, You work so many miracles in the Blessed Sacrament, work this one more—draw me entirely to Yourself. You more than deserve that I should belong entirely to You, and You also wish it. Give me strength to love You with all my heart.

Give the goods of this world to whomsoever You please. I renounce them all. I long only for Your love. It is for that alone I am seeking and will continue to seek. I love You, my Jesus; grant that I may always love You. I ask for nothing more.

Aspiration: My Jesus, when shall I really love You?

SPIRITUAL COMMUNION (page 2).

Visit To Our Lady

"Mother most amiable!" How pleasing to me is that beautiful title which your devout children give you, my most sweet Queen! Indeed, my Lady, you are most lovable. Your beauty has captivated God Himself. *The King shall greatly desire thy beauty.* (Ps. 44:12). St. Bernard says that your very name is so dear to those who love you that when they hear it or utter it themselves, their desire to love you grows. That I should love you, O Mother most amiable, is only right. But I am not satisfied merely to love you. I wish, both now on earth and later on in Heaven, to be, after God, the one that loves you most. If this desire is too bold, it is your own lovableness and the

special love you have shown me that are
to blame. If you were less lovable, my
desire to love you would be less. Accept, O
Lady, this desire of mine, and since God is
pleased so much when anyone loves you,
obtain for me from Him, as a sign of your
acceptance, the love for you that I am
asking.

Aspiration: Mother most amiable, I love you
very much.

PRAYER: "MOST HOLY VIRGIN . . ." (page 3).

Eighteenth Visit

PRAYER: "MY LORD JESUS CHRIST . . ." (page 1).

ONE day, in the valley of Josaphat,
Jesus will be seated on a throne of
majesty. But now, in the Blessed
Sacrament, He is seated on a throne of love.
If, to show his love for him, a king were to
go and live in the village of a poor shepherd, how ungrateful would that shepherd
not be if he did not often go to visit him
in spite of the fact that he knew the king
was most anxious to see him frequently,

and, indeed, that it was for this very purpose he had come to live there at all.

Ah, my Jesus, well do I know that it is because of Your love for me that You have come to dwell in the Sacrament of the Altar! Were it possible for me, I should wish to remain in Your presence day and night. If the Angels, astounded at the love You have for us, remain always around You, O my Lord, it is only reasonable that I, who realize that it is for my sake You are on the altar, should please You by remaining in Your presence to praise Your goodness and the love You have for me. *I will sing praise to Thee in the sight of the angels; I will worship towards Thy holy temple and I will give glory to Thy name, for Thy mercy, and for Thy truth.* (Ps. 137:1, 2).

O God, present in the Blessed Sacrament, O Bread of Angels, O heavenly Food, I love You. But, no more than You, am I satisfied with my love. I do love You, but I love You too little. My Jesus, make me appreciate the beauty and the goodness of the One I love. Make my heart banish all its earthly loves and leave itself entirely open to Your divine love. In order to fill my heart with love for You and to unite Yourself wholly to me, You descend from Heaven onto our altars every day. It is only fair that I should think of nothing else but of loving, adoring and pleasing You. I love You with all my heart. And if You wish to reward me for this love, give me a love that is ever greater, ever more fervent still, a love that will make me wish to please You more and more.

Aspiration: Jesus, my love, give me love for You!

SPIRITUAL COMMUNION (page 2).

Visit To Our Lady

Just as the sick poor, abandoned by everybody because of their misery, find shelter only in charitable institutions, so do the most wretched sinners, though rejected by all, find a refuge in the mercy of Mary. For God has placed her in the world to be for sinners a shelter, or, as St. Basil says, a public hospital. For this reason St. Ephrem calls her the Refuge of Sinners. Therefore, my Queen, if I have recourse to you, you cannot reject me on account of my sins. Rather, the more wretched I am, the greater is the claim I have on your protection, because God Himself has made you the refuge of the most

forsaken. And so, O Mary, I have recourse
to you now. I place myself under your mantle. You are the refuge of sinners; be the
hope of my salvation. If you reject me, to
whom shall I have recourse?

Aspiration: Mary, my refuge, save me!

PRAYER: MOST HOLY VIRGIN . . ." (page 3).

Nineteenth Visit

PRAYER: "MY LORD JESUS CHRIST . . ." (page 1).

TO be in the company of a dear friend
is a pleasure for everyone. Shall not
we, in this valley of tears, find it a
pleasure to remain in the company of our
best Friend, that Friend who can do for
us everything that is good, who loves us
most tenderly, and who, for that very reason, dwells with us always? See how we
can converse at will with Jesus—we can
open our hearts to Him, lay our wants
before Him and ask Him for His grace. In
a word, in the Blessed Sacrament we can
speak to the King of Heaven with the
utmost confidence and without any feel-

ing of restraint. Sacred Scripture tells us that Joseph was only too happy when God, by means of His grace, descended into his prison to comfort him. *She went down with him into the pit, and in bands she left him not.* (*Wis.* 10:13, 14). But we are far more privileged still. Always with us in this vale of tears we have our God made Man, who is full of tenderness and pity for us, and who, by His Real Presence, helps us all the days of our lives. What a consolation it is to a poor prisoner to have a loving friend who comes to visit him, who consoles him, gives him hope, helps him and tries to have him set free once again. Here in the Blessed Sacrament is our loving Friend, Jesus Christ, who says, to encourage us: *Behold, I am with you all days.* (*Matt.* 28:20). See Me here, He says, all yours. I have come down from Heaven into your prison for the express purpose of consoling you, of helping you and setting you free. Welcome Me, remain with Me always, cling to Me. In this way you will forget your troubles. And later on you will come with Me to My Kingdom, where I shall make you perfectly happy.

O God, O Love that is beyond our understanding, since You bend down so much toward us as to leave Heaven in order to live near us on the altar, I am determined to visit You often. I wish to enjoy as often as I possibly can Your most sweet presence, which is the cause of the happiness of the Saints in Heaven. Oh, if only I could remain in Your presence always, to adore You and make You acts of love! I beg of You to arouse me from my lethargy whenever, because of coldness or preoccupation with worldly affairs, I neglect to visit You. Enkindle in my heart a great desire to remain always near You in the Blessed Sacrament. Ah, my loving Jesus, if only I had always loved You! If only I had always pleased You! I console myself with the thought that I still have the opportunity of loving and pleasing You, not only in the next life, but in this life also. I wish to do so; I wish to love You, my Love, my Treasure, my All. I will love You with all my heart.

Aspiration: My God, help me to love You!

SPIRITUAL COMMUNION (page 2).

Visit To Our Lady

The saintly Bernardine de Bustis says: "Do not despair, O sinner, but go with confidence to Our Lady. You will find her hands filled with grace and mercy." "And remember," he adds, "that this Queen, who is so full of sympathy, is more anxious to help and assist you than you yourself can be that she should do so." O my Lady, I always thank God for having taught me about you. I should be unfortunate indeed if I did not know of you, or if I were to forget you. My very salvation would be in danger. O my Mother, I bless you, I love you. And so great is the confidence I have in you that I entrust my soul to your keeping.

Aspiration: O Mary, happy is the one who knows you and puts his trust in you!

PRAYER: "MOST HOLY VIRGIN . . ." (page 3).

Twentieth Visit

PRAYER: "MY LORD JESUS CHRIST . . ." (page 1).

In that day there shall be a fountain open to the house of David and to the inhabitants of Jerusalem: for the washing of the sinner. (Zach. 13:1).

THIS fountain, which Zacharias foretold would be accessible to everybody, is Jesus in the Blessed Sacrament. To it we can go, whenever we please, to wash from our souls all the stains of sin that remain after the faults of the day. When any one of us commits a fault, is there any better remedy than immediately to go to Jesus in the Blessed Sacrament?

Yes, my Jesus, I am determined to do this always, for I realize that not only do the waters of this fountain of Yours cleanse me; they also give me light. They give me strength to avoid sin and to accept cheerfully whatever goes against me. They make me burn with love for You. I know that is why You long for me to visit You, and why You reward with so many graces the visits of those who love You. My Jesus, come!

Cleanse me of all the faults I have committed today. I am very sorry for them because they have displeased You. Strengthen me against falling again by giving me a great desire to love You. If only I could remain near you always, as did Your servant, Mary Diaz, in the time of St. Teresa! The Bishop of Avila gave her permission to live in the tribune of a church. There she remained almost always in the presence of the Blessed Sacrament, which she used to speak of as her Neighbor. Whenever the Venerable Brother Francis of the Infant Jesus, a Discalced Carmelite, passed near a church where the Blessed Sacrament was reserved, he always called in to pay a visit. He said it was not becoming for a man to pass the door of a friend's house without calling in to exchange a word of greeting. But a mere word did not satisfy him; he always remained in the presence of His beloved Master as long as ever he could.

O my God, You Who are Infinite Goodness, it is in order that I might love You that You have instituted the Blessed Sacrament and that You remain always on the altar. I realize, too, that that is why You have made my heart capable of loving You

very much. Why is it, then, that I am so
ungrateful as not to love You, or that I love
You as little as I do? No, it is not just or
fair that one who is so good and lovable as
You should receive so little love. At least
the love You have for me deserves a greater
return of love than I am giving You. You
are God, and are infinite. I am a creature,
without worth of my own. If I were to spend
all my energies in Your service, if I were
to die for You, it would be very little, seeing that You have died for me and left Yourself in the Blessed Sacrament for my sake,
and that You sacrifice Yourself every day
on the altar just because of the love You
have for me. You deserve a very great love;
I wish to love You very much. Help me, my
Jesus, to do that which gives You so much
pleasure, that which You want so much of
me—help me to love You!

Aspiration: My Beloved to me and I to my
Beloved!

SPIRITUAL COMMUNION (page 2).

Visit To Our Lady

What great confidence does not St.
Bernard inspire in me when I have recourse

to you, my most dear and lovable Queen! He says that you do not examine the merits of those who have recourse to your mercy, but that you are ready to help everyone who prays to you. And so, if I pray to you, in your kindness and mercy you will hear me. Listen, then, to what I have to ask you. I am a poor sinner who deserves Hell a thousand times over. I wish to change my life. I wish to love my God, whom I have offended so seriously. I dedicate myself to you as your servant; to you I give myself, poor as I am. Save, then, one who is no longer his own but belongs to you. Do you understand, my Lady? I feel sure that you do and that you will hear my prayer.

Aspiration: O Mary, I belong to you; save me!

PRAYER: "MOST HOLY VIRGIN . . ." (page 3).

Twenty-First Visit

PRAYER: "MY LORD JESUS CHRIST . . ." (page 1).

Wheresoever the body shall be, thither will the eagles also be gathered together. (Luke 17:37).

BY this body the Saints usually understand that of Jesus Christ. And the eagles they interpret as being detached souls who, like eagles, rise above the things of earth and fly toward Heaven, which is at once the object as well as the dwelling place of all their thoughts and desires. These souls find their heaven-on-earth wherever Jesus in the Blessed Sacrament is present. And so they seem never to grow tired of being with Him. St. Jerome says that if eagles come flying from a great height and distance to get their food once they perceive it, all the more ought we to fly to Jesus in the Blessed Sacrament, for He is the food of our souls. And so the Saints, in this valley of tears, have always come to this heavenly fountain of the Blessed Sacrament, just as thirsting deer would to running water in a valley. The

Jesuit, Fr. Balthasar Alvarez, no matter what work in which he was engaged, used often to look toward where he knew the Blessed Sacrament was reserved. Very often he visited It, and sometimes he remained there the whole night through. He wept when he saw the palaces of noblemen filled with people who paid homage merely in the hope of gaining some worthless favor, and thought how abandoned were the churches, where God Himself, the Lord of the world, who is really rich—but in eternal treasures—dwells in our midst on a throne of love. Religious, he said, are specially favored since, even in their own houses, they can visit this great Lord in the Blessed Sacrament whenever they wish, night or day—a thing that people in the world cannot do.

Since, then, my most loving Lord, You invite me so lovingly to come to You, in spite of my wretchedness and the ingratitude I have shown You for Your love, I will not lose heart at the sight of my unworthiness. I come to You, but I ask that You change me completely. Drive from my heart every love that is not for You, every desire that does not please You, every thought that is not directed to You. My Jesus, my Love, my Treasure, my All, I wish to satisfy You alone, I wish to please only You. You are the only one who deserves all my love. You only will I love with all my heart. Make me detached from everything, my Lord, and bind my heart to Yourself alone. But bind me so tightly that I may never again be able to separate myself from You, either in this life or in the next.

Aspiration: My most sweet Jesus, do not ever permit me to be separated from You!

SPIRITUAL COMMUNION (page 2).

Visit To Our Lady

Denis the Carthusian calls the Blessed Virgin the advocate of all sinners who have recourse to her. Since, then, it is your duty, O great Mother of God, to defend the most guilty sinners who call upon you, see, I am now at your feet. I have recourse to you, and I say with St. Thomas of Villanova: "O kindly Intercessor, act now in accordance with the duty entrusted to you." It is true that I am most guilty in the eyes of God, for, in spite of the many favors and graces granted me, I have offended Him very much. But the evil is already done. You can save me. You have only to tell God that you are defending me. I shall then be forgiven and shall be saved.

Aspiration: My dear Mother, save me you must!

PRAYER: "MOST HOLY VIRGIN . . ." (page 3).

Twenty-Second Visit

PRAYER: "MY LORD JESUS CHRIST . . ." (page 1).

HAVE *you seen Him whom my soul loveth?* (*Cant.* 3:3) was the question put to all whom she met by the spouse in the Book of Canticles when she was searching for her loved one and could not find him. At that time the Son of God had not yet come on earth. But now, if one who loves Jesus is searching for Him, she can always find Him in the Blessed Sacrament. Of all sanctuaries, Ven. Father John Avila said he could neither find, nor wish for, a more delightful one than a church where the Blessed Sacrament was reserved.

O infinite love of my God, You deserve

an infinite love in return! How has it happened, my Jesus, that You have humbled Yourself so far as to hide Yourself under the appearance of bread, and only to be able to live among men and to unite Yourself to their hearts? O God Incarnate, You are unsurpassed in humility because You are unsurpassed in love. How can I fail to love You with all my heart when I realize how much You have done to win my love? I love You very much, and because I do, I prefer the doing of Your will to all my own pleasures, all my own interests. To please You, my Jesus, my God, my Love, my All, is pleasure for me. Make me long to remain continually in Your sacramental presence, to welcome You and to keep You company. I should certainly be ungrateful were I not to accept Your kind invitation. Destroy in me, O Lord, every attachment to created things. It is Your will that You Yourself, my Creator, should be the only object of all my longings, of all my love. I love You, most lovable goodness of my God. I ask nothing of You but Yourself. I do not desire my own pleasure; to please You is all I wish. That will be enough for me. O Jesus, accept this good desire of a sinner who now wishes to love You. Help me with Your grace, and

grant that as, up to the present, I have
been enslaved by sin, so, for the future, I
may be the slave of Your love.

Aspiration: O Jesus, my Treasure, I love
You more than every other treasure!

SPIRITUAL COMMUNION (page 2).

Visit To Our Lady

My most gracious Lady and Mother, by
committing sin I have rebelled against
your Son. But I am sorry, and I appeal to
your mercy to obtain forgiveness for me.
Do not say that you have not the power.
St. Bernard says that you are the media-
trix who obtains forgiveness for us. It is
your duty to help those who are in danger, for St. Ephrem calls you the helper
of those in peril. And who, my Lady, is in
greater danger than I? I have lost God and
have certainly deserved Hell. I do not
know if God has yet forgiven me. I may
lose Him again. But you can obtain everything for me, and it is through you that I
hope for every favor, for pardon, perseverance and paradise. I hope, in Heaven,
to be among those of the blessed who will
be loudest in praising your mercy because

you will have saved me by your prayers. *Aspiration:* I will sing the mercy of Mary for eternity. I will sing of it forever and ever. Amen.

PRAYER: "MOST HOLY VIRGIN . . ." (page 3).

Twenty-Third Visit

PRAYER: "MY LORD JESUS CHRIST . . ." (page 1).

MANY people endure great physical weariness and expose themselves to a certain amount of danger in going to visit the places in the Holy Land where our loving Saviour was born, suffered and died. But there is no need for us to make as long a journey as that or to face any danger. That same Saviour is close to us. He lives in the church, which is only a short distance from our homes. St. Paulinus says that if pilgrims returning from the Holy Land consider it a great privilege to bring back a little dust from the crib or from the tomb of Jesus, how fervent should we not be when we actually visit Jesus Himself, really present in person in the

Blessed Sacrament, seeing that we can do so without experiencing the weariness and danger of a pilgrimage.

In one of her letters, a religious to whom God had given an intense love for the Blessed Sacrament expressed, among other things, the following sentiments: "I realize that everything good in me comes from the Blessed Sacrament. I have offered and consecrated myself entirely to my Sacramental Jesus. I know that numberless graces are not granted simply because people do not go to Jesus in the Tabernacle. His desire to distribute graces from this throne of Love is very great. O holy Mystery! O Sacred Host! Where, if not in the Blessed Sacrament, does God show the greatness of His power? For the Sacred Host is the expression of all that God has ever done for us. We ought not to be envious of the lot of the blessed, for here on earth we have the very same God as they, only that to us He shows even greater marvels of His love. Try to get everybody with whom you speak to give himself completely to Jesus in the Tabernacle. I say this because the Blessed Sacrament of the Altar makes me forget myself. I cannot help but speak always of It, because It deserves to be loved so very much. I do not know what to do for Jesus in the Blessed Sacrament." There the letter ends.

O Seraphim, you remain always before the Tabernacle, burning with love for your Lord and mine, even though it was because He loved me, rather than you, that He wished to leave Himself there at all. O loving Angels, let me too burn with love. Enkindle in my heart your love so that I too may burn with love for Him.

O my Jesus, make me realize how great is the love You have for men, so that, having such love before my eyes, I may ever desire more and more to love You and please You. I love You, dear Jesus, and I wish to love You always, and that solely to give You pleasure.

Aspiration: My Jesus, I believe in You, I hope in You, I love You and I give myself to You.

SPIRITUAL COMMUNION (page 2).

Visit To Our Lady

O Virgin Mary, so worthy of love, St. Bonaventure calls you the Mother of orphans, and St. Ephrem speaks of you as the receiver of orphans. These helpless orphans are none other than poor sinners who have lost God. See, then, I have recourse to you, O Mary most holy. I have lost my Father; but you are my Mother and must help me find Him. In this great misfortune of mine I call you to my assistance. Help me! Shall I remain unconsoled? No, indeed. For Innocent III asks: "Who that ever called upon her for help was not kindly heard by her?" Who that had recourse to you was ever lost? It is only he that does not fly to you that is lost. And so, my Queen, if you wish me to be saved, help me always to call upon you and to trust in you.

Aspiration: My own Mary most holy, give me confidence in you!

PRAYER: "MOST HOLY VIRGIN . . ." (page 3).

Twenty-Fourth Visit

PRAYER: "MY LORD JESUS CHRIST . . ." (page 1).

Verily Thou art a hidden God. (*Is.* 45:15).

IN no other work of God's love is the truth of these words shown so clearly as in the adorable mystery of the Most Holy Sacrament, where our God is completely hidden. When the Eternal Word took flesh, He hid His divinity and appeared on earth as a man. But in remaining with us in the Blessed Sacrament, Jesus hides even His humanity and, as St. Bernard points out, appears only under the form of bread in order to show us how tender is the love He has for us.

Seeing this excessive tenderness of Your love for men, O my beloved Redeemer, I am astonished and do not know what to say. In this Sacrament Your love for them goes so far as to make You hide Your majesty and lessen Your glory. Here in the Tabernacle Your only occupation seems to be to love men and to show them that You love them. And what gratitude do they show You in return, O great Son of God?

Allow me to say that Your love for men is too great, O my Jesus, because I see that You prefer their welfare to Your own glory. And were You not aware of the great amount of contempt to which this loving plan of Yours would expose You? I see what You Yourself saw long ago—that the majority of men do not adore You nor appreciate You in the Blessed Sacrament as You deserve. I know that these very men have often gone so far as to trample on the consecrated Hosts, to throw them into water and into fire. And I know, too, that the greater part even of those who do believe in You, O God, instead of making reparation for such insults by their loyalty, offend You still more by their irreverence when they come to the church or leave You all alone on the altar, which is sometimes without even a lamp or the necessary ornaments.

Oh, my most sweet Saviour, I only wish that I could wash with my tears, and even with my blood, those places where, in this Sacrament, Your love and Your Sacred Heart have been so greatly insulted. But if that wish is not granted me, at least, my Lord, I wish and am determined to visit You often, so as to adore You as I today adore You, and to make reparation for all the insults You receive in this divine mystery at the hands of men. O Eternal Father, accept this small honor which I, the most unworthy of men, offer You today in reparation for the insults offered to Your Son in the Blessed Sacrament. Accept it in union with that honor of infinite value which Jesus Christ gave You on the Cross and still gives You every day in the Blessed Sacrament. O my Sacramental Jesus, if only I could fill the hearts of all men with love for You!

Aspiration: O loving Jesus, make Yourself known, make Yourself loved.

SPIRITUAL COMMUNION (page 2).

Visit To Our Lady

O Lady most powerful, in spite of my fears for my eternal salvation, I feel great confidence when I have recourse to you. I know, on the one hand, that you, my Mother, are so endowed with grace that St. John Damascene speaks of you as a sea of grace; St Bonaventure as a treasury of grace; St. Ephrem as the source of grace and every consolation; and St. Bernard as the perfection of everything that is good. I realize, on the other hand, that you are so anxious to help us that you are hurt when we do not ask you for graces.

O most wise and merciful Queen, rich in spiritual gifts, you know the wants of my soul better than I myself do; you love me far more than ever I could love myself. Do you know, then, the grace I am asking of you now? Obtain for me the grace that you know to be the best for my soul. Ask God for this favor and I shall be satisfied.

Aspiration: My God, grant me the graces which Mary asks of You for me!

PRAYER: "MOST HOLY VIRGIN . . ." (page 3).

Twenty-Fifth Visit

PRAYER: "MY LORD JESUS CHRIST . . ." (page 1).

ST. PAUL, praising the obedience of Jesus Christ, says that He obeyed His Eternal Father even when it meant death for Himself: *becoming obedient unto death.* (*Phil.* 2:8). But here in the Blessed Sacrament He has gone even further than that. Here He has wished to obey not only His Eternal Father, but also a mere man, and that not only until death, but as long as ever the world will last. He has become obedient, we can say, even to the end of the world. At the bidding of a man, the King of Heaven comes down onto the altar, and He dwells there, it would seem, just to obey men. *And I do not resist.* (*Is.* 50:5). He remains there motionless. He allows Himself to be placed wherever men wish, to be exposed in the Monstrance or locked in the Tabernacle. He allows Himself to be carried wherever men take Him, whether it be into houses or through the public streets. He allows Himself to be given in Holy Communion to anyone who comes to receive Him, whether he be in the state of grace or in mortal sin. St. Luke tells us that while He lived on earth He obeyed Our Lady and St. Joseph. In the Blessed Sacrament, He obeys as many men as there are priests in the world. *And I do not resist.*

O Heart of my Jesus, in Whose love all the Sacraments, but especially that of the Altar, find their source, allow me to speak to You now. Gladly would I give You as much honor and glory as You give to the Eternal Father by remaining in the Tabernacle in our churches. I know that here on this altar You still love me just as much as when You closed Your life in anguish on the Cross. O divine Heart, teach all those who do not know You about Yourself. By Your merits, free, or at least relieve, the suffering souls in Purgatory. They already belong to You for eternity. I adore You, I thank You, I love You, together with all the souls in Heaven or on earth who are loving You at this moment. O most pure Heart, purify my heart of every attachment to things of earth and fill it with Your holy love. O most sweet Heart, take entire possession of my heart, so that for the future it may belong entirely to You, making it possible for me to say: *Who shall be able to separate us from the love of God, which is in Christ Jesus, our Lord?* (*Rom.* 8:39).

O most sacred Heart, write upon my heart all the bitter sorrows You endured for so many years on earth because of Your love for me, so that, when I see them, I may long for suffering, or at least bear with patience all the sorrows of life, just because I love You. Most humble Heart of Jesus, give me a share in Your humility. Most meek Heart, impart Your gentleness to me. Take away from my heart everything that does not please You. Make it entirely Your own, so that my only wish may be to do Your will. In a word, grant that my only object in life may be to obey, love and please You. I realize that You have put me under an infinite obligation to You. I can never repay You. To sacrifice myself entirely to You and wear myself out in Your service will be but a small attempt at repayment. *Aspiration:* O Heart of Jesus, You are the only King of my heart!

SPIRITUAL COMMUNION (page 2).

Visit To Our Lady

The earthly ark in which Noe escaped from the destruction of the world by water prefigures Our Lady. For St. Bernard says that she is the heavenly ark that will save our souls from eternal destruction if only we take refuge in it in time. But Hesychius says that the ark of Mary is stronger and can hold more people than that of Noe. The number of men and beasts sheltered and saved in his ark was small. But Mary, who is our ark, shelters everyone who takes refuge under her mantle and brings them all to certain safety. We should indeed be very unfortunate if we had not Mary. And yet, O my Queen, how many, in spite of that, are lost! And why? Because they do not go to you for refuge. Would anyone ever be lost if only he went to you?

Aspiration: Grant, O Mary most holy, that all of us may always have recourse to you.

PRAYER: "MOST HOLY VIRGIN . . ." (page 3).

Twenty-Sixth Visit

PRAYER: "MY LORD JESUS CHRIST . . ." (page 1).

Rejoice, and praise, O thou habitation of Sion: for great is He that is in the midst of thee, the Holy One of Israel. (Is. 12:6).

O GOD, what a joy should it not be to us men, with what hope and love should it not inspire us, to know that in our own very land, in our own churches, quite near our own homes, the true God, the Holy of Holies, is really living and present in the Blessed Sacrament of the Altar! That God whose very presence makes the Saints in Heaven happy! That God who is

Love itself! St. Bernard tells us that it is not so much that God loves us or gives the gift of love, as that He is actually Love itself. So the Blessed Sacrament is not merely a sign indicating love, but is Love itself, because It is God Himself, who, on account of the very great love He has for us whom He has created, calls Himself, and really is, Love itself: *God is Love (Charity).* (*1 John* 4:16).

But I hear You complaining, O my Sacramental Jesus, that You came on earth to be our guest, to help us and do good for us, and that we have not made You welcome. *I was a stranger, and you took me not in.* (*Matt.* 25:43). You are right, O Lord: it is quite true. And I am among the ungrateful ones who have left You all alone and have not even come to visit You. Punish me as You please, but do not deprive me of Your presence, which is the punishment I deserve. I wish to make up to You for the rude and discourteous way I have treated You. For the future, not only will I visit You often, but I will stay with You for as long as I can. O most merciful Saviour, grant that I may be faithful to You and that my example may inspire others to keep You company in the Blessed Sacrament. I hear the Eternal Father say: *This is My beloved Son, in whom I am well pleased.* (*Matt.* 17:5). If God finds in You a source of happiness for Himself, shall not I, too, who am only a worthless creature of His, find my happiness in this valley of tears in living with You? O consuming fire of love, destroy in my heart every attachment to things created, for they only can make me unfaithful to You; they only can separate us. You have the power to destroy these attachments if You wish; *Lord, if Thou wilt, Thou canst make me clean.* (*Matt.* 8:2). You have already done so much for me; do this too. Drive from my heart every love that is not in keeping with Your love. I give myself entirely to You. This very day I dedicate all that remains of my life to loving the Blessed Sacrament. O my Sacramental Jesus, it is You Who must be my comfort. You must be the one for me to love during life and in the hour of death, when, I trust, You will come to be my Food and Guide for my journey to Your holy kingdom. That is my hope. Oh, may it be so!

Aspiration: When, O my Jesus, shall I see Your beautiful face?

SPIRITUAL COMMUNION (page 2).

Visit To Our Lady

Mother most holy, you are the cure for all our troubles. It is you who obtain for us strength when we are weak. In you we find a door through which we can escape from the slavery of sin. With you we have assurance of peace. In this our life of exile, you are our comfort. In a word, it is through you that we obtain divine grace and reach to God Himself. Our sins have driven Him far away from us. You are the bridge He uses to return once more to live in our souls by His grace.

Aspiration: O Mary, you are the source of my strength, of my freedom from sin, of my peace of mind and of my salvation.

PRAYER: "MOST HOLY VIRGIN . . ." (page 3).

Twenty-Seventh Visit

PRAYER: "MY LORD JESUS CHRIST . . ." (page 1).

IN the Office of the Blessed Sacrament the Church sings: "There is no other people, however great, whose gods come as near to it as our God does to us." When the pagans heard to what an extent the love of our God went, they cried out: "Oh, how good a God is this God of the Christians!" And yet, in spite of the fact that the pagans invented their gods according to their own whims, read their fables and the accounts of the many gods they did invent and you will find that they never even dreamed of imagining a god who could love men as much as our true God actually does. This God of ours, to show how much He loves those who adore Him and to fill them with the richness of grace, has performed a very miracle of love. He has become our constant companion, remaining night and day hidden on our altars, quite incapable, it would seem, of tearing Himself away from us even for a moment. *He hath made a remembrance of His wonderful works.* (Ps. 110:4).

O my most sweet Jesus, it was to satisfy Your intense longing to be near us and
with us always that You wished to work
the very greatest of Your miracles. Why,
then, do men shun You? How can they live
far away from You for so long and visit You
so seldom? How comes it that they get so
tired in Your presence that a quarter of an
hour seems an age? O Jesus, how great is
Your patience! Yes, my Lord, I know the
reason. Your patience is great because Your
love for us men is great. That it is which
makes You live always among us, ungrateful though we are.

O my God, up to the present I have been
among these ungrateful ones. Do not allow
that to be so for the future. Give me a love
that corresponds to what You deserve and
to what I owe You. There was a time when
I too grew tired in Your presence, either
because I did not love You at all or because
I loved You only too little. But if You help
me by Your grace to love You very much, I
shall not any longer find it tiresome to stay
even the whole length of day and night at
Your feet in the Blessed Sacrament.

O Eternal Father, I make You the offering of Your own Son. Accept Him in my
name, and because of His merits, grant me

a love for the Blessed Sacrament so burning and tender that I may constantly turn my mind to some church where Jesus dwells, to think of Him and to long earnestly for the time when I shall be free to go and take pleasure in His company. *Aspiration:* My God, for the love of Jesus, give me a deep and tender love for the Blessed Sacrament!

SPIRITUAL COMMUNION (page 2).

Visit To Our Lady

It is built with bulwarks: a thousand bucklers hang upon it, all the armour of valiant men. (Cant. 4:4). This Tower of David of which the Holy Ghost speaks in the Book of Canticles is Mary. O Mary most holy, you are a most powerful means of defense for all who are engaged in spiritual battles. O most dear Lady, how constantly do my enemies attack me, trying to deprive me of the grace of God and of your protection! But you are my source of strength against them. You are only too pleased to do battle for those who trust you. Seeing, then, that I trust you and confide in you so very much, I ask you to defend me and fight for me.

Aspiration: Mary, Mary, your name is my means of defense.

PRAYER: "MOST HOLY VIRGIN . . ." (page 3).

Twenty-Eighth Visit

PRAYER: "MY LORD JESUS CHRIST . . ." (page 1).

Seeing that God has given us His own Son, why should we be afraid that He will refuse us anything that is for our good? *How hath He not also, with Him, given us all things?* (*Rom.* 8:32). We know that God the Father has given everything He has to Jesus Christ: *The Father had given Him all things into His hands.* (*John* 13:3). And so, let us ever thank the goodness, the mercy and the generosity of our loving God who, in giving us Jesus in the Blessed Sacrament, has made us rich in grace and in everything that is good. *In all things you are made rich in Him . . . so that nothing is wanting to you in any grace.* (*1 Cor.* 1:5, 7).

O Saviour of the world, O Word Incarnate, I can regard You as being my very own, as belonging entirely to me, if only I wish it so. But can I say that I belong entirely to You, as You wish me to? Ah, my Lord, do not give the world a chance of seeing such an exhibition of ingratitude or wrongheadedness—that I should not belong entirely to You when You want me so much. Do not allow that to happen. If it has been the case in the past, do not let it be so in the future. With all my heart I consecrate myself entirely to You today. For this life and for eternity I consecrate to You my will, my thoughts, my actions and sufferings, my life itself. As a victim consecrated to loving You, I renounce everything created. I belong completely to You. Make my heart burn with flames of love for You. I have no wish that creatures should share my heart's love any longer. The fact that You have given me proof of Your love for me, even when I did not love You, gives me great confidence that You will accept me now that I do really love You and, because of that love, consecrate myself to You.

Eternal Father, I offer You today all the virtues, the actions and the love of the Heart of Your dear Jesus. Accept them on my behalf, and through His merits, which are now really mine since He has made them over to me, grant me the graces He asks of You. By means of these merits I wish to thank You for the many times You have shown me mercy. With them I wish to pay off the debt I owe You by my sins. I trust that they will obtain for me every grace I need—forgiveness, perseverance, Heaven and, more than all others, the crowning grace of loving You. I am well aware that it is I myself who place the obstacles to all these graces. But You can remedy that too. I ask You to do so, for the love of Jesus Christ. He has promised: *Whatsoever you shall ask the Father in my name, that will I do.* (John 14:13). You cannot refuse me then. Lord, the only desire I have is to love You, to give myself to You without reserve and to be no longer ungrateful to You as I have been up to the present. Look down on me and hear my prayer. Grant that this may be the day of my turning completely to You—turning in such a way that I may nevermore fail to love You. I love You, my God! I love You, O Infinite Goodness! I love You, Who are my Happiness, my Life, my very All.

Aspiration: O Jesus, You who are everything to me, You long for me, and I for You.

SPIRITUAL COMMUNION (page 2).

Visit To Our Lady

O most sweet and holy Mother Mary, how relieved do I not feel in my troubles, how consoled in my worries, how strengthened in temptation when I think of you and call on you to help me! The Saints were perfectly right in calling you "the shelter of those who are in trouble," "the consoler of the afflicted," "the consolation of those who are in sorrow."

My own Mary, do console me. I realize that I am weighed down with sin and surrounded by enemies. I have little virtue and am cold in my love for God. Do console me, O Mother, and let your consolation consist in making me begin a new life, one that will really be pleasing to your Son and to you.

Aspiration: Change my heart, O Mary, my Mother, change my heart. It is in your power to do so.

PRAYER: "MOST HOLY VIRGIN . . ." (page 3).

Twenty-Ninth Visit

PRAYER: "MY LORD JESUS CHRIST . . ." (page 1).

Behold, I stand at the gate, and knock.
(*Apoc.* 3:20).

O MOST loving Shepherd, the love You have for Your sheep was not satisfied when You sacrificed Your life for them on the altar of the Cross. That love made You leave Yourself on the altar in our churches, hidden in the Blessed Sacrament, so that You might be always near us, able to knock at the door of our hearts to gain entrance there. If only I could take the same delight in Your closeness to me as did the Spouse in the Book of Canticles! She says: *I sat down under His shadow, whom I desired.* (*Cant.* 2:3). O my dear Jesus, if I loved You, if I really loved You, I too should wish never to have to leave the foot of the altar, day or night. There, near where You hide Your majesty under the visible appearance of bread, I should place myself, and I too should experience the happiness and heavenly consolation that souls who love You find there. Draw me to Yourself by the attraction of Your beauty and of the love for us that You show in the Blessed Sacrament. *Draw me: we will run after Thee to the odour of Thy ointments. (Cant.* 1:3). Yes, my Saviour, I will leave creatures and all the pleasures of earth to hasten to You in the Sacrament of the Altar. *As olive plants, round about Thy table. (Ps.* 127:3). What fruits of virtue do not these souls, who in their love remain before the Tabernacle, produce in the sight of God! They are like fruitful olives.

I am ashamed to come before You, O my Jesus, because of my complete want of virtue. You have commanded that everybody who comes to the altar to honor You should bring a present: *Thou shalt not appear empty before Me. (Ex.* 23:15). What, then, am I to do? Am I not to come before You anymore? Ah, no. That would not please You. Poor as I am, I still will come to You. You Yourself must provide me with the gifts You ask of me. I am well aware that it is not only to reward those who love You that You remain in the Blessed Sacrament. You wish also to provide from the riches of Your grace for those who are poor in virtue.

Very well; let us begin from today. I adore You, O King of my heart. You are the true lover of men, the Shepherd who loves His sheep beyond all believing. To this throne of Your love I now come. Since I have no other present to give You, I offer You my poor heart, that it may be consecrated entirely to loving You and to doing Your will. With this heart of mine I am able to give You my love, and I really wish to love You as much as I can. Take it, then, to Yourself, and bind it to doing Your will entirely, so that from today onward, I may be able to rejoice in the fact that I, like Your dear disciple St. Paul, am a prisoner in the chains of Your love. *I, Paul, the prisoner of Jesus Christ. (Eph.* 3:1). Unite me, my Lord, to Yourself. Make me forget about myself so that one day I may have the happiness of becoming completely detached from everything, even myself, so as to find You and love You forever. I love You, my Jesus in the Blessed Sacrament. It is to You I bind and unite myself. Help me to love You more; and never depart from me. *Aspiration:* My Jesus, You alone are enough for me.

SPIRITUAL COMMUNION (page 2).

Visit To Our Lady

St. Bernard speaks of Mary as being the safe road which will lead us to the Saviour and to our own salvation. Since it is true, O Queen, that you are the one who takes our souls to God, you cannot expect me to come nearer to God unless you carry me in your arms! Carry me, carry me! And if I resist you, carry me in spite of myself. By the sweet attraction of your love, do all in your power to force my heart and my rebel will to give up created things and to seek only God and His holy Will. Show all Heaven the greatness of your power. Your mercy has made you perform many a miracle of grace. Let it make you perform yet another—that of bringing close to God one who has lived far from Him.

Aspiration: O Mary, it is in your power to make me a saint. I trust in you to obtain for me this grace.

PRAYER: "MOST HOLY VIRGIN . . ." (page 3).

Thirtieth Visit

PRAYER: "MY LORD JESUS CHRIST . . ." (page 1).

Why hidest Thou Thy face? (Job 13:24).

JOB was afraid when He saw that God hid His face. But to see Jesus Christ hiding His majesty in the Blessed Sacrament should not make us afraid, but rather fill us with greater confidence and love than ever. For His real purpose in remaining hidden under the appearance of bread on the altar is to increase our trust and confidence in Him and to make His love for us more evident. If this King of Heaven dwelt on the altar in all His majesty and glory, would we ever have the courage to approach Him with confidence or open our hearts to Him?

O my Jesus, how great must have been the love which prompted You to institute the Blessed Sacrament—to hide Yourself under the appearance of bread so that men might love You, and that anyone who wished might find You here on earth! The Prophet Isaias was right when he said that we should make known to the whole world the extent to which God's love for us goes: *Make His works known among the people.* (*Is.* 12:4). O most loving Heart of my Jesus, worthy of holding the love of all creatures, Heart that is ever aflame with the purest love, consume me entirely in that flame, and give me a new life of love and holiness. Unite me to Yourself in such a way that I may never be separated from You in the future. O Heart, ever an open refuge for souls, receive me! O Heart, torn in sorrow on the cross for the sins of the world, give me true sorrow for my sins! I know that in the Blessed Sacrament You still have the same love for me that You had when dying on Mount Calvary. You still have a burning desire to unite me completely to Yourself. Can I possibly hold back any longer from giving myself entirely to Your love and Your wishes? Through Your merits, my beloved Jesus, wound my heart with Your love and unite my will to Yourself in everything. Today, with the help of Your grace, I resolve to give You all the pleasure I possibly can, by trampling underfoot all human respect, all my natural likes and dislikes, my own convenience, everything which may keep me from pleasing You perfectly. Help me, my God, to carry out this resolution in such a way that, from today, all my actions and thoughts, all my affection, may be completely in keeping with Your holy Will. O Love of God, drive every other love from my heart. O Mary, my hope, your prayers are all-powerful with God. Obtain for me the grace to love Jesus faithfully until death.

Aspiration: Who shall separate me from the love of Christ?

SPIRITUAL COMMUNION (page 2).

Visit To Our Lady

St. Bernard tells us that Mary's love for us cannot exercise any more power on our behalf than it actually does, or be greater than it actually is. And so she is always ready to pity us because of her love and to help us because of her power.

Yes, my most pure Queen, you have great sympathy for us and great power to help us. It is in your power to save us all, and that is your earnest wish. I will pray to you, then, today and every day, in the words of the saintly Blosius: "O Lady, protect me in my struggles and strengthen me when I am beginning to waver." O God, how many

temptations have I not still to overcome
before my death! O Mary, my hope, you who
are my refuge and my source of strength,
do not ever allow me to lose the grace of
God. And I, on my part, promise always to
run to you immediately when temptation
comes to me, and to say:

Aspiration: Help me, O Mary! Mary, help
me!

PRAYER: "MOST HOLY VIRGIN . . ." (page 3).

Thirty-First Visit

PRAYER: "MY LORD JESUS CHRIST . . ." (page 1).

WHAT a wonderful sight it must
have been to see our dear
Redeemer that day He sat down
by the side of the well, tired out after His
journey, waiting, in all gentleness and charity, for the coming of the Samaritan woman
that He might win her from sin and save
her soul. *Jesus, therefore, sat on the well.*
(*John* 4:6). It is exactly in this way that
the very same Jesus lives now with us all
day long on the altar, where He has come

from Heaven itself. Every altar is a well of grace where He waits for souls and invites them to stay with Him, at least for a while, that He may win them over to loving Him perfectly. From every altar where the Blessed Sacrament is, He seems to speak to us all and say: Why do you shun Me? Why do you not come to visit Me, seeing that I love you so much and that it is for your sake I remain here in this humble state? Of what are you afraid? It is not to pass judgment that I have come on earth, but to do good and to save all those who have recourse to Me. That is why I have hidden myself in this Sacrament of Love. *I came not to judge the world, but to save the world.* (*John* 12:47).

Let us try to realize that just as Jesus Christ in Heaven is *always living to make intercession for us,* as St. Paul says (*Heb.* 7:25), so in the Blessed Sacrament too He is always, night and day, interceding for us, offering Himself as a victim to His Eternal Father to win us God's mercy and numberless graces. And so the holy Thomas à Kempis says that we ought to come to Jesus in the Blessed Sacrament without fear of being punished and that we should speak to Him without any feeling of restraint, just as we would to a dear friend.

Since, then, my hidden Lord and King, You wish me to regard You as a friend, with complete confidence I shall open my heart to You and say: O my Jesus, You who love souls so much, I well realize the injustice that men do You. You love them, but they do not love You. You are kind and good to them, and they despise You. You wish them to hear Your voice, but they will not listen. You offer them graces, and they refuse them. O my Jesus, is it not true that at one time I also was ungrateful and displeased You as they? Unfortunately it is only too true! But, during the days of life that still remain to me, I wish to make amends. By doing all that I possibly can to please You and console You, I hope to make reparation for the displeasure I have caused You. Tell me, O Lord, what Your will is. I wish to carry it out without any reservation. Make it known to me through obedience, and I hope to be able to do it. My God, I sincerely promise you from today forward that, whenever there is a choice, I will always choose what I know to be more pleasing to You, even though that choice should cost me the loss of everything—of parents, friends, esteem, health, even of life itself. Let me lose them all, if only it be Your will. Happy is the loss indeed, O my God, when everything is sacrificed to satisfy Your Heart. I love You, my good God, You Who are more worthy of love than anything else that is good. And in loving You I unite my heart to the love of the Seraphim. I unite it to the Heart of Mary, to the Heart of Jesus. I love You with all my heart. I will love only You and will do so always.

Aspiration: My God, my God, I belong to You, and You to me.

SPIRITUAL COMMUNION (page 2).

Visit To Our Lady

Blessed Amadeus says that Mary, our Queen, is always in the presence of God, pleading with Him and interceding for us by her powerful prayers. For, he tells us, she is well aware of our worries and our difficulties, and, being the gracious Lady she is, she has a mother's sympathy for us and helps us with a mother's love.

My most loving Mother and my intercessor with God, you can see at this moment my soul's anxiety. You see my danger, and you are praying for me. Pray, pray, and do not ever cease to pray until you see me in Heaven, thanking you for having won my salvation. O most sweet Mary, the saintly Blosius tells us that, after Jesus, you are the sure and certain means of salvation for your faithful servants. This is the grace I am asking of you now—grant me the happiness of being your faithful servant until I die, so that after death I may go to praise you in Heaven, where I shall be certain of remaining at your sacred feet forevermore, as long as God is God.

Aspiration: O Mary, my Mother, grant that I may belong to you always.

PRAYER: "MOST HOLY VIRGIN . . ." (page 3).

Benediction of the Most Blessed Sacrament

O Salutaris

O Salutaris Hostia,

Quae coeli pandis ostium,

Bella premunt hostilia,

Da robur, fer auxilium.

Uni Trinoque Domino

Sit sempiterna gloria:

Qui vitam sine termino,

Nobis donet in patria.
Amen.

O Saving Victim, opening wide
The gate of Heav'n to man below,
Our foes press on from every side;
Thine aid supply, Thy strength bestow.

To Thy great name be endless praise,
Immortal Godhead One in Three;
O grant us endless length of days
In our true native land with Thee. Amen.

Tantum Ergo

Tantum ergo Sacramentum
Veneremur cernui.

Down in adoration falling,
Lo, the Sacred Host we hail;

Et antiquum documentum
Novo cedat ritui;

Lo, o'er ancient forms departing,
Newer rites of grace prevail;

Praestet fides supplementum
Sensuum defectui.

Faith for all defects supplying
Where the feeble senses fail.

Genitori, Genitoque,

To the everlasting Father,

Laus et jubilatio:

And the Son Who reigns on high,

Salus, honor, virtus quoque
Sit et benedictio;

With the Holy Ghost proceeding
Forth from each eternally;

Procedenti ab utroque

Salutation, honor, blessing,

Compar sit laudatio.
Amen.

Might and endless majesty. Amen.

V. Panem de coelo praestitisti eis.
(Alleluia).

V. You have given them bread from Heaven. (Alleluia).

R. Omne delectamentum in se habentem. (Alleluia).

R. Having in itself every sweetness.
(Alleluia).

Oremus

Deus, qui nobis sub Sacramento mirabili passionis tuae memoriam reliquisti, tribue, quaesumus: ita nos Corporis et Sanguinis tui sacra mysteria venerari, ut redemptionis tuae fructum in nobis jugiter sentiamus: Qui vivis et regnas in saecula saeculorum. Amen.

Let Us Pray

O God, Who under a wonderful Sacrament has left us a memorial of Your Passion, grant us, we beseech You, so to venerate the sacred mysteries of Your Body and Blood, that we may ever enjoy the fruit of Your Redemption: Who live and reign forever and ever. Amen.

The Divine Praises

Blessed be God.

Blessed be His holy Name.

Blessed be Jesus Christ, true God and true man.

Blessed be the Name of Jesus.

Blessed be His Most Sacred Heart.

Blessed be His Most Precious Blood.

Blessed be Jesus in the Most Holy Sacrament of the Altar.

Blessed be the Holy Ghost, the Paraclete.

Blessed be the great Mother of God, Mary most holy.

Blessed be her holy and Immaculate Conception.

Blessed be her glorious Assumption.

Blessed be the Name of Mary, Virgin and Mother.

Blessed be St. Joseph, her most chaste Spouse.

Blessed be God in His Angels and in His Saints.

Ant. Adoremus in aeternum Sanctissimum Sacramentum.

Ant. Let us adore forever the Most Holy Sacrament.

Laudate Dominum omnes gentes: laudate eum omnes populi:

Quoniam confirmata est super nos misericordia eius: et veritas Domini manet in aeternum.

V. Gloria Patri, et Filio, et Spiritui Sancto.

R. Sicut erat in principio, et nunc et semper, et in saecula saeculorum. Amen.

Praise the Lord all ye nations: praise Him all ye people.

For His mercy is confirmed upon us: and the truth of the Lord remains forever.

V. Glory be to the Father, and to the Son, and to the Holy Ghost.

R. As it was in the beginning, is now, and ever shall be, world without end. Amen.

Ant. Adoremus in aeternum Sanctissimum Sacramentum.

Ant. Let us adore forever the Most Holy Sacrament.

NOTES

NOTES

NOTES

NOTES

NOTES

NOTES

NOTES

Prices subject to change.

Old World and America. (Grades 5-8) *Furlong* 21.00
Old World and America Answer Key. *McDevitt* 10.00
Miraculous Images of Our Lord. *Cruz* 16.50
Ven. Jacinta Marto of Fatima. *Cirrincione* 3.00
Ven. Francisco Marto of Fatima. *Cirrincione,* comp. . . . 2.50
Is It a Saint's Name? *Dunne* 3.00
Prophets and Our Times. *Culleton* 15.00
Purgatory and Heaven. *Arendzen* 6.00
Rosary in Action. *Johnson* 12.00
Sacred Heart and the Priesthood. *de la Touche* 10.00
Story of the Church. *Johnson et al.* 22.50
Summa of the Christian Life. 3 Vols. *Granada* 43.00
Latin Grammar. *Scanlon & Scanlon* 18.00
Second Latin. *Scanlon & Scanlon* 16.50
Convert's Catechism of Cath. Doct. *Geiermann* 5.00
Christ Denied. *Wickens* 3.50
Agony of Jesus. *Padre Pio* 3.00
Tour of the Summa. *Glenn* 22.50
Three Ways of the Spir. Life. *Garrigou-Lagrange* 7.00
The Sinner's Guide. *Ven. Louis of Granada* 15.00
Radio Replies. 3 Vols. *Rumble & Carty* 48.00
Rhine Flows into the Tiber. *Wiltgen* 16.50
Sermons on Prayer. *St. Francis de Sales* 7.00
Sermons for Advent. *St. Francis de Sales* 12.00
Sermons for Lent. *St. Francis de Sales* 15.00
St. Dominic's Family. (300 lives). *Dorcy* 27.50
Life of Anne Catherine Emmerich. 2 Vols. (Reg. 48.00) . 40.00
Manual of Practical Devotion to St. Joseph. 17.50
Mary, Mother of the Church. *Documents* 5.00
The Precious Blood. *Faber.* 16.50
Evolution Hoax Exposed. *Field* 9.00
Devotion to the Sacred Heart. *Verheylezoon* 16.50
Chats with Converts. *Forrest* 13.50
Passion of Jesus/Its Hidden Meaning. *Groenings* 15.00
Baltimore Catechism No. 3. . . . . 11.00
Explanation of the Balt. Catechism. *Kinkead* 18.00
Spiritual Legacy of Sister Mary of the Trinity. 13.00
Dogmatic Theology for the Laity. *Premm* 21.50
How Christ Said the First Mass. *Meagher* 21.00
Victories of the Martyrs. *St. Alphonsus* 13.50

Prices subject to change.

Practical Comm./Holy Scripture. *Knecht.* (Reg. 40.00) . 30.00
Sermons of St. Alphonsus Liguori for Every Sun. 18.50
True Devotion to Mary. *St. Louis De Montfort* 9.00
Religious Customs in the Family. *Weiser* 10.00
Sermons of the Curé of Ars. *Vianney.* 15.00
Revelations of St. Bridget of Sweden. *St. Bridget* 4.50
St. Catherine Labouré of/Miraculous Medal. *Dirvin* 16.50
St. Therese, The Little Flower. *Beevers* 7.50
Purgatory Explained. (pocket, unabr.) *Fr. Schouppe* 12.00
Prophecy for Today. *Edward Connor* 7.50
What Will Hell Be Like? *St. Alphonsus Liguori* 1.50
Saint Michael and the Angels. *Approved Sources* 9.00
Modern Saints—Their Lives & Faces. Book I. *Ball* 21.00
Our Lady of Fatima's Peace Plan from Heaven 1.00
Divine Favors Granted to St. Joseph. *Pere Binet.* 7.50
Catechism of the Council of Trent. *McHugh/Callan.* . . . 27.50
Padre Pio—The Stigmatist. *Fr. Charles Carty* 16.50
Fatima—The Great Sign. *Francis Johnston* 12.00
The Incorruptibles. *Joan Carroll Cruz* 16.50
St. Anthony—The Wonder Worker of Padua 7.00
The Holy Shroud & Four Visions. *Fr. O'Connell* 3.50
St. Martin de Porres. *Giuliana Cavallini* 15.00
The Secret of the Rosary. *St. Louis De Montfort* 5.00
Confession of a Roman Catholic. *Paul Whitcomb* 2.50
The Catholic Church Has the Answer. *Whitcomb* 2.50
I Wait for You. *Sr. Josefa Menendez* 1.50
Words of Love. *Menendez, Betrone, etc.* 8.00
Little Lives of the Great Saints. *Murray.* 20.00
Prayer—The Key to Salvation. *Fr. M. Müller.* 9.00
Alexandrina—The Agony and the Glory. 7.00
Life of Blessed Margaret of Castello. *Fr. W. Bonniwell.* . 9.00
St. Francis of Paola. *Simi and Segreti.* 9.00
Bible History of the Old and New Tests. *Schuster* 16.50
Dialogue of St. Catherine of Siena 12.50
Dolorous Passion of Our Lord. *Emmerich* 18.00
Textual Concordance of the Holy Scriptures. PB. 35.00

A Plenary Indulgence

A *Plenary* Indulgence is the remission before God of *all* the temporal punishment due to be suffered for already-forgiven sins.

A Catholic, being in the state of grace, can gain a Plenary Indulgence by many different prayers and works of piety, including:

Making a visit to the Blessed Sacrament to adore It for at least one half hour.

In addition to the Visit, these three conditions are required:
1. Confession;
2. Holy Communion;
3. Prayer for the Holy Father's intentions. (One Our Father and one Hail Mary suffice.)

The three conditions may be fulfilled several days before or after the performance of the prescribed work; it is fitting, however, that Communion be received and the prayer for the intention of the Holy Father be recited on the same day the work is performed.

In addition, to gain a Plenary Indulgence, a person's mind and heart must be free from all attachment to sin, even venial sin.

If one tries to gain a Plenary Indulgence, but fails to fulfill all the requirements, the indulgence will be only partial.

From the leaflet "How to Gain a Plenary Indulgence," TAN, Imprimatur ✠ Most Rev. Thomas G. Doran, Bishop of Rockford, March 31, 1998.